CASTLE.

THE SCOTTISH SOLDIER

London Scottish Detachment at the parade to mark the granting of the Freedom of the City of Aberdeen to the Gordon Highlanders Regiment, 20th August, 1949.

DEDICATION

For my son, Timothy, whose
ancestors, English and Scots,
have been soldiers.

Members Sergeants' Mess, The Royal Scots Greys (2nd Dragoons). Aldershot, May, 1936.

THE SCOTTISH SOLDIER

An illustrated social and military
history of Scotland's fighting men
through two thousand years.

STEPHEN WOOD

Keeper of the Scottish United Services Museum in
Edinburgh Castle.

ARCHIVE PUBLICATIONS LIMITED
in association with

The National Museums of Scotland

© 1987 Stephen Wood
ISBN 0948946 11 3
Published by Archive Publications Ltd
Carrington Business Park, Urmston, Manchester.
All Rights Reserved
Typesetting by Witwell Ltd, Liverpool.
Production by Richardson Press.

3

His Majesty King George VI as Colonel-in-Chief of the Scots Guards. King's Birthday Parade, 1938.

Jacket Design by Val Sasson.
Layout by Clive Hardy
Additional photographic research by Clive Hardy and Nigel Arthur.

THE SCOTTISH SOLDIER

FOREWORD

by
Lieutenant-General Sir Norman Arthur K.C.B.
General Officer Commanding the Army in Scotland
and the Governor of Edinburgh Castle.

This history of the Scottish soldier is the fruit of an accomplished pen, a witty style of writing and, undoubtedly, of wide and well-informed research. The reader will be led briskly through the story from the early days, of the Scottish spearman and of the wild charge of Highlanders in battle, to the forming, in the 17th and 18th centuries, of our great, and well-known, regular regiments. Their history follows until it reaches the grim accounts of the huge and tragic sacrifices of Scottish soldiers in the two world wars of this century. A shrewd insight to the Scottish soldier of today concludes the book.

Of course, in 200 pages, such a vast record must be broadly told and must make its points simply. *The Scottish Soldier* does just this, and perhaps the most fundamental, and unusual, point is made as early as the introduction – soldiers are popular in Scotland! The reader receives the clearest possible framework from which, as his interest is stimulated, he may pick his field of further reading, whether it be in uniforms or weapons, in the Regiments or the Divisions or in one historic period or another. Stephen Wood's chapter titles alone tell us much. They portray most distinctively and, in at least one case, movingly, the important eras which the story covers. A mass of illustration excites immediate interest and a full bibliography guides the reader to further study.

This is the story of countless servants of Scotland and of the British Empire, and of the famous bodies in which for the past 300 years, and still, they have served. Impressed man and conscript, yeoman, volunteer and career soldier, all merit their inclusion in this enduring brotherhood. The names of many of them, Highlanders and Lowlanders, countrymen and men in tens-of-thousands from the towns and cities, can be found on stones of granite throughout Scotland.

June 1987.

ACKNOWLEDGEMENTS

John Donne's observation that No Man is an Island applies especially to authors and particularly to those of books such as this. For their help and assistance in a variety of ways I wish to record my gratitude to the following people.

For their help in providing the illustrations I have to thank Ian Larner, Doreen Moyes and Joyce Smith of the National Museums of Scotland; Marion Harding and Lesley Smurthwaite of the National Army Museum; Susan Payne of Perth Museum and Art Gallery; Alex Buchanan of the Historic Buildings and Monuments Division, Scottish Development Department and Elaine Proctor of the Scottish National Portrait Gallery.

For their assistance I have to thank my colleagues William Boag, Charles Burnett, David Caldwell, Allan Carswell, Wynne Harley, June McDonald and Gordon Richardson. I also owe debts of gratitude to John Hayward, Donna McDonald and Lieutenant-Colonel Ian Shepherd RHF.

For making the book possible I have to thank my Director, Robert Anderson, and my colleague Sheila Brock.

For her persistently cheerful and characteristically efficient aid in so many areas, not least in the compilation of the bibliography and the selection of many important illustrations, I have to thank my valued colleague Helen McCorry.

For translating my manuscript into typescript I have to thank Helen Forrest.

For their advice and guidance I have to thank Lieutenant-General Sir Norman Arthur KCB, General Officer Commanding the Army in Scotland and Governor of Edinburgh Castle and Colonel Michael Ashmore CBE, commanding The Scottish Division. Their assistance and the companionship of other Scottish soldiers, past and present, of all ranks has contributed significantly to what little understanding I can claim of the subject of this book.

Finally, I owe a greater debt than I can ever repay to my Muse, who has provided advice, criticism, solace and inspiration. Her identity is my business.

CONTENTS

INTRODUCTION

Contrary to popular belief, even in Scotland, the Scottish soldier resists and defies generalisations. Highlander and Lowlander, cavalryman and infantryman, gnarled old sweat and fresh-faced recruit, hero and coward, victor and vanquished: all have been represented by the description so glibly given and so infrequently qualified.

There were few soldiers in Britain before the seventeenth century. Plenty of armed men, warriors or men-at-arms, but few soldiers in the sense of disciplined, organised bodies of uniformed, regimented, professional, full-time individuals owing allegiance to a Sovereign or other Head of State. Such people barely existed in Britain between the departure of the soldiers of Rome and the Restoration of the Stuart monarchy in 1660. Although the New Model Army of the late 1640s was the predecessor of the modern British Army it was an English Army.

There is now nothing unique about the Scottish soldier. It is possible that, for a brief period during the second half of the eighteenth century, the Highland soldier might qualify for such an assessment, but such uniqueness as existed was weakened by the wars in America and India and finally destroyed by those against France. As the ancient Highland societies were changed by repression, exploitation and emigration during the late eighteenth and early nineteenth centuries, so their young men ceased to be different from their rural peers elsewhere in the country and The King's red coat masked any few remaining idiosyncrasies.

The Lowland soldier had never been any different to his English, Irish or Welsh comrades. Only when, after centuries of being despised, Scotland and things Scottish became fashionable in the nineteenth century did the Lowland regiments adopt an outward appearance that marked them – by the standards of that time and the present – as Scottish. In adopting tartan and quasi-Highland accoutrements they were aping the section of society that their forebears had feared, hated and gone to great lengths to exterminate. Such is one of the many contradictions represented by Scotland.

In any historical study of soldiers, one is persistently struck by the realisation of how little actually changes. This 'timelessness of soldiering' applies as much to Scotland's soldiers as it does to those of America, Russia or any other nation with a military past. Things improve of course: pay rises, punishments change and the business of killing or being killed involves differing degrees of technology and varying types of skill. Aside however, from the clothes that they wear and the weapons which they use (which are, after all, only modifications of the sewn skins and the pointed stick) soldiers remain much the same type of animal from century to century. One can talk to soldiers today, of all ranks, and discover attitudes that would not, allowing for developing speech patterns, sound out-of-place if expressed by their predecessors of decades, or even centuries, before.

Most persistent of these attitudes, hardly surprisingly, is the belief that one's section, or platoon, or company, or battalion, or regiment, or country, is better than any other equivalent identifiable body. It is on the basis of such belief that success is built, that motivation is achieved and, at bottom, that wars are won. Scottish soldiers are as full of such beliefs as are all other soldiers; it is part of their conditioning to be so. Such attitudes are not, of course, confined to soldiers. In some schools, the concept of House loyalty is imprinted at an early age; elsewhere in society it is more frequent that such allegiances and resulting beliefs will attach themselves to Association Football teams. In Scotland, where – for a variety of reasons – the soldier is closer to the civilian population than elsewhere in the United Kingdom, allegiance to a football team is often accompanied by one to a regiment: the local team and the local regiment. This does not make the soldiers better soldiers, although it may once have done, but it does mean that Scotland possesses a factor which makes it unique among Western industrialised nations: soldiers are popular in Scotland.

This makes Scotland unique, it does not necessarily make her soldiers so. Neither was it always the case. In fact, it is a phenomenon of the last hundred years and one which owes much to the invention of a Scottish consciousness based upon wholly fraudulent interpretations of historical facts.

Such interpretations are, I hope, no part of this book. Even assuming that I have been successful in identifying those most elusive of spirits, the proven and indisputable historical facts, there will be many who disagree with my interpretation of them. The revelation that I am an English civilian may explain much, even though the risk exists that such a revelation may set members of the Clan Gregor to selecting the sharpest item of cutlery from the knife rack and looking up the latest kidnap exchange rates. The further revelations that this book is intended to appeal to a popular, and not an academic, audience; that it was researched and written in three months and that its author is well aware of the fact that it does no more than scratch the surface of a fascinating and complex story may calm those who look for academic or lofty philosophical argument in the following pages. Intended to accompany the exhibition *The Story of the Scottish Soldier 1600–1914* at the Scottish United Services Museum, it is the author's intention that this book should also stand alone as a realistic tribute to those who have made its compilation possible: the officers and men of the Scottish regiments of the British Army, past, present and future.

Stephen Wood,
Scottish United Services Museum,
Edinburgh Castle.

June, 1987

CHAPTER ONE

SPEARMEN OF SCOTLAND

1st century A.D. to 1603

Scotland grew to nationhood slowly and painfully. The peoples who, at various times, occupied the land we now know as Scotland fought each other and among themselves because such conflict was about personal survival at its most basic, about land ownership and about power.

In the centuries which preceded that of the seventeenth, when the story of Scotland's soldiers really begins, there was little concept of soldiering as a trade or profession simply because the bulk of the able-bodied male population were all potential warriors. There were professional men-at-arms of course, who served a chief as part of his retinue, but these bodyguards were not large enough to constitute an army. At best, they could frighten a few tenants, impose a kind of arbitrary justice and generally bolster their chief's position by the grandeur of their finery and ferocity of their appearance. In time of national or regional war these retainers would form the nucleus of hastily-raised armies of civilians, the majority of whom would have some practical knowledge of the use of the primitive weapons with which they were armed. The strength of these armies lay primarily in their weight of numbers.

At the other end of the social and military scale, from the peasant plucked from the plough and armed with a pointed stick, was the knight. Gradually clad, as the centuries progressed, in protective clothing of increasing sophistication and expected, as part of his education. To be proficient in the use of his weapons, the knight represented the officer class among the armies of the medieval period.

The first professional soldiers as such to be seen in Scotland were those of Rome. They can be described as soldiers since they were subject to a system of discipline, organised into regiments, dressed in a kind of uniform manner and operated within codified forms of regulation. Although Roman influence in Scotland ebbed and flowed from the first century A.D. until the withdrawal of the legions from Britain in the fifth century, there is no apparant evidence that the organisation of the Roman armies left any mark on the tribal societies in occupation of the various parts of Scotland. This is not surprising since the role of the Roman armies, as the mailed fist of the Empire, was quite different to that of the war-bands organised in opposition to them by the local chiefs and tribal leaders in Scotland.

The effect of the withdrawal of Roman military protection from Britain during the fifth century A.D. was less marked in Scotland than it was in England. Roman rule had been under sustained, and increasingly successful, attack from the tribes who were gradually becoming known collectively as *Picts* for a considerable time. Hadrian's Wall, itself something of an admission of defeat, had long since ceased to act as an effective barrier against the wild men of the north.

In the six centuries between the end of the Roman occupation and the Norman invasion, the history of Scotland was marked by large and small-scale contests for land ownership. Such contests were characterised by conflict. When the Romans left, Scotland was occupied by two peoples whom it is convenient to label *Picts* and *Britons*; the *Picts* north of the Forth estuary, the *Britons* in the south-west. In addition to these two differing, yet related, groups, the *Scots* threatened western Scotland from the north of Ireland and the *Angles* were encroaching into the south-east. Each of the four groups of peoples had substantial warrior elements within their societies, each were hungry for land or desperate to defend what they had, and none were prepared to give way without a fight. Anglian ambitions north of the Tay estuary were set back considerably by their crushing defeat at the hands of the Pict chief Brude at the battle of Nechtansmere in 685. Nechtansmere is near the present-day town of Dunnichen in Angus but, apart from knowing its location and that the Anglian king Ecgfrith and large numbers of his men were killed, we know little about the conduct of the battle or its participants.

One of the earliest depictions of Scottish warriors, that of Pictish cavalry and infantry on a stone in the churchyard of Aberlemno near Forfar in Angus, shows that both horse- and foot-soldiers were armed with comparatively short spears and small shields. It is reasonable to suppose that these represented the essential weapons of the ordinary fighting Scot at the time. It is probable that such expensive and status-giving weapons as swords were confined to the professional warriors and it is likely that mounted warriors were a type of elite force within the armies of the period.

By the time of the Viking invasions of the ninth century Scotland was divided into three. The Picts and Scots had been united by Kenneth MacAlpine in 843 and occupied the area north of the rivers Clyde and Forth; the Angles occupied Lothian and the Britons had managed to hang on in Strathclyde. While each of the three areas seems to have accepted the existence of the others, there can be little doubt that there would have been considerable frontier tension and sporadic skirmishing. The Viking influence on each of the kingdoms was considerable and, because it was largely imposed by violence – at first at any rate, involved further decades of conflict. The Vikings, or at least those who spearheaded the attacks on Britain, were professional warriors and, as the assault troops of a new invasion, they inspired the same reaction among the residents of Britain as had previous invaders.

It is questionable whether the Vikings influenced the weapons of the inhabitants of Scotland much since, although they are known to have been great exponents of the use of the axe in warfare, axes certainly existed in Scotland before the ninth century as domestic tools. There is, after all, little difference between the use of a sharp tool in its domestic environment and the use of the same implement as an offensive weapon. Whatever the truth of the matter, Viking warriors employed the axe to a great extent in war and, in modified forms, it remained a relatively popular weapon in the part of Scotland most influenced by Viking settlement, the North, until beyond the medieval period. These warriors, who seem – for the most part – to have come from Norway and who settled in Orkney, Shetland and the north and north-west of mainland Scotland, were organised in much the same way as were the warriors already in residence. They were armed, depending upon their station in the tribal hierarchy, with axes, short spears or swords and protected themselves with shields, helmets (of conical form rather than those adopted by Hollywood Vikings and adorned with horns or wings) and jackets or jerkins of loosely-connected metal plates. They seem, as were the residents of Scotland, to have been competent rather than renowned archers and their swords were things of great beauty as well as fearsomely efficient.

It might be thought that the successful invasion of England by the French descendants of Norsemen in 1066 would have had little influence on the kingdoms in the north of Britain but this was far from the case. The Norman victory at Hastings in 1066 helped, eventually, to produce the Scotland that we know today and influenced the development of the Scottish, as well as the English, soldier to a considerable extent. The gradual establishment of the form of rule known as feudalism in England combined with the exertion of Anglo-Norman influence northward during the eleventh and twelfth centuries to extend that system of government to the more accessible parts of Scotland. Feudalism, the system by which individuals held land granted to them by the King in return for payment of taxes, loyalty and, especially, rendering of military service, worked well in a united nation such as England where an entirely new nobility which owed everything to the King could be implanted. In an area such as Scotland, which remained riven by discord, which operated a variety of differing systems of hierarchical rule, which was resentful of outside – or even central – impositions of authority and of which vast

5

Pictish stone in Aberlemno churchyard depicting warriors. about 500 AD.

6

Scottish axe-head, about 1200 AD.

9

areas were largely impenetrable, a system such as feudalism could only be partially successful. This proved to be the case. It was successfully imposed upon the accessible parts of Scotland gradually throughout the twelfth and thirteenth centuries by imported Norman nobles who rapidly became part of the Scottish hierarchy. Castles were built, private bands of retainers were maintained and armed with examples of the latest developments in weapon technology and, inevitably, the local magnates began to flex their newly-developed muscles in contest with each other and, occasionally, with their Kings.

The warriors used by these magnates were primarily their tenants, called from the cultivation of their land, hastily armed and equipped with rudimentary armour. They were liable to serve as warriors as part of their obligation to their landlord in return for their plots of land and protection by him and his full-time retainers from the forces of neighbouring landlords. The weapon with which they were

most likely to be armed was the spear, for the length and use of which the Scots became famous throughout the medieval period, and fortunate ones might be issued with a long mail shirt, or *hauberk*, and a metal helmet. The more talented and fit men would be trained as archers and most categories of warriors would be armed with an axe for both functional and killing purposes.

The unification of Scotland in the thirteenth century, following the final subjugation of the Viking threat from the North at the Battle of Largs in 1263, presented England with a cohesive threat on her northern boundary. The attempts of England and her Kings to exert either influence or dominion over Scotland from the thirteenth century inevitably led to the beginnings of frequent armed conflict between the two nations. Although these wars were accompanied by internal faction-fighting within both countries, and numerous instances on both sides of self-seeking fifth column activities, they did serve in Scotland both to concentrate the

Viking sword hilt, about 1100AD

Grave image of Reginaldus of Islay, from the island of Texa, about 1380.

Left: Scottish Knight's sword, about 1450.

9

10

Right: The Battle of Bannockburn 1314, from the *Scotichronicon*, Corpus Christi College, Cambridge.

Below: The tomb effigy of John Houston of Houston in Houston Church, Renfrewshire, dating from about 1450.

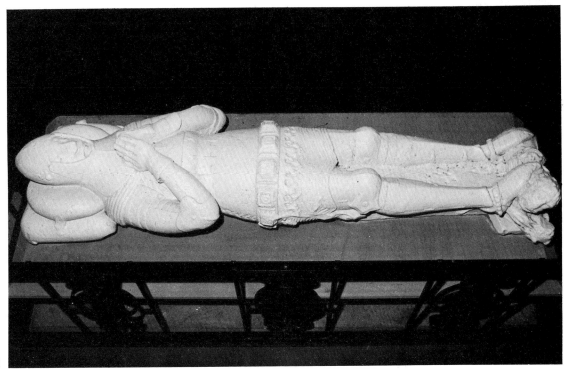

11

minds of her Kings and nobles and, as all wars do, to aid the development of military technology and tactics.

In the two and a half centuries between the Battle of Stirling Bridge in 1297 and that of Pinkie in 1547 the armies of Scotland and England clashed on fourteen separate occasions and, while Scotland claimed eight notable victories, most cataclysmic and long-lasting in effect were the defeats of her arms at Flodden, Solway Moss and Pinkie, all in the first half of the sixteenth century against the resurgent England of Henry VIII.

The long spear, or pike, was as characteristically the weapon of the medieval Scottish infantryman as was the longbow of the English. Pikes, rarely of less than five metres long and frequently more than five and a half, were used consistently throughout the period and, when their users were properly drilled, deployed and supported by the lightly-armed Scots cavalry, the manoeuvrable hedges that they formed, known as *schiltrons*, were impenetrable and potentially lethal. Unlike the English and continental armies, Scotland's armies were not renowned for their use of heavily-armoured cavalry although, of course, her knights were as proficient in the use of their lances, swords, axes and maces as any of their peers. Neither were Scots archers worthy of comparison with those who served in the English armies and who dealth such efficient death at Flodden and Pinkie. There were similarities however, primarily in the enforced encouragement that had to be given to the practice of archery in both England and Scotland where it tended to be superseded, whenever possible, by the less strenuous pastimes of football and, especially in Scotland, of golf.

Very little armour appears to have been made by Scots for Scots in Scotland and, certainly, almost none survives today. Although armourers were encouraged, and even imported, much of the basic body armour of the Scottish warrior, even as late as the Battle of Flodden in 1513 was either imported plate armour or locally-manufactured *jacks* (heavy, quilted jerkins reinforced with small plates).

Of great significance to the history of warfare during the medieval period, and of no less relevance to the military history of Scotland, was the invention of gunpowder and its use first in cannon and subsequently in hand-held firearms. The use of gunpowder changed the military landscape. It necessitated alterations in castle design and changes of mind about their defensive, and therefore strategic, use; it eventually banished armour from the battlefield and sounded the death knell of the bow. Kings of Scotland were quick to realise the potential of artillery, and cannon are known to have been used by their armies before the end of the fourteenth century. While much ordnance was imported from the foundries of France and the Low Countries, like the great bombard *Mons Meg* still resident in Edinburgh Castle, Scotland rapidly became noted for the manufacture of both iron and bronze cannon in foundries in the Castles of Edinburgh and Stirling during the late fifteenth and early sixteenth centuries.

Supported by artillery, and horsemen equipped with swords and lances, armed with his spear or his long-shafted axe, his knives and his shield, the Scottish warrior of the

medieval period was liable for, in theory at least, up to forty days military service per year. He was responsible for the provision and maintenance of his own weapons by c.1500 and had to produce them at regular intervals for their state of readiness to be checked. This system had evolved from the old-style feudalism and was to last until the creation of a Standing Army in the mid-seventeenth century. In Highland Scotland, of course, feudalism as such had never really penetrated but, in its realities and essentials, the clan system that applied there was much the same, particularly as regards the liability of the individual for military service.

As the sixteenth century progressed, however, the division between Highlands and Lowlands became gradually more marked as Scottish society disintegrated under internal and external pressures. Periods of firm government alternated with chaos; periods of unity with the growth of faction and self-interest among the Scottish nobility. Private armies marched and counter-marched across Scotland, sometimes in the cause of the preservation of the Old Religion, sometimes in the name of the New, invariably – at bottom – representing personal ambition in the guise of religious or national principle. Parts of the Highlands were tamed, momentarily, by King James V in the late 1530s and the Auld Alliance with France was periodically rejuvenated in order to counter the resurgent power of Tudor England. It was a time of regencies, of civil war, of the Reformation of the Church and of the gradual draining away of Scottish independence.

Throughout it all the armed men of Scotland were kept even busier than in previous years. Inspired by prospects of loot or of settling old scores, fired by religious fervour or threatened with summary justice, the men of Scotland followed their various spiritual and temporal leaders back and forth across a country in crisis. Many left to seek employment overseas rather than live under a Reformed Church at home, many fled with prices on their heads and many died, frequently at the hands of their own countrymen.

The story of the armed men of Scotland was drawing to a close at the same time as was the sixteenth century and the life of Elizabeth I of England. The story of the Scottish soldier was about to begin.

12

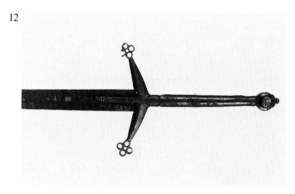

The original *claidheamh mor*, a two-handed sword about 1520.

CHAPTER TWO

MERCENARIES AND REGULARS

1603 to 1688

When King James VI of Scotland succeeded Queen Elizabeth I of England he became King James I of England and united the two Crowns. The actual governments of England and Scotland were not to be united for another century and so, for the period covered in this chapter, we should remember that England and Scotland were still very much separate nations.

Scotland in 1603 was a fairly lawless place, although the accessible areas had quietened down after the civil war of the previous century. James had tamed the nobility where he could get at them and even in the Borders, where the political division between the two nations was no more than a line on a map, the great families had been brought more-or-less to heel. Legislation, the attractions of life at court and the use of a mounted police force had dissuaded all but the most hardened of the Border reivers from continuing their activities. The Lowland and coastal areas had discovered prosperity and were beginning to enjoy a long period of domestic peace. James regarded the Highlands with fascinated horror and divided them between the merely barbarous and the utterly barbarous; here The King's Writ was at best tenuous. Commissions of Fire and Sword, a spine-chilling phrase exhorting the use of both, were issued to clan chiefs favoured because their barbarity was mere rather than utter or because they were far-sighted or self-seeking enough to see how their futures lay. The Campbells fought the MacDonalds on behalf of James, the MacKenzies fought whoever they were paid to fight and everyone fought the MacGregors.

The propensity of Scots to fight each other was being exploited by foreign rulers too. Scotland had joined those countries readily able to supply soldiers for anyone who could pay by the mid-sixteenth century and the Kings of France had had a Scottish company in their Bodyguard since 1440. The religious and political conflicts that historians know as the Thirty Years War merely increased an already existing traffic when they began in 1618. During the fiercest fighting at the end of the 1620s, when huge armies manoeuvred across central Europe, King Gustavus Adolphus of Sweden was believed to have had 20,000 Scots in his forces, and he thought highly of them. Gustavus Adolphus was the champion of the Protestant cause until his death at the Battle of Lützen in 1632 and one of the foremost soldiers of his age. France represented the leading Catholic protagonist and, at one point, 10,000 Scots served her King, inevitably facing fellow

countrymen on the same field of battle. Religious scruples seem to have mattered little to some of the Scots who fought in these wars of religion; it is known that Catholic Scots fought for the Protestant cause but whether the threat of the Inquisition prevented the reverse from being true is less apparent. Gustavus Adolphus lost one of his best Scottish commanders when he questioned the motives of the Catholic John Hepburn who promptly changed sides and took his fellow countrymen into the service of France. Hepburn's action resulted, in 1633, in the raising of the regiment which is senior of all British line infantry regiments and now known as The Royal Scots (The Royal Regiment); it remained principally in the French service until the 1670s.

Hepburn was one among many Scots who rose to eminence in the Swedish service. Although he died a Marshal of France in 1636, many of his equally-experienced countrymen survived to return to Britain at the end of the 1630s when civil wars threatened to convulse first Scotland and then England. Pre-eminent among the returning Scots who were forced to make decisions of conscience and to take sides during the escalating tension between Parliament and King in both Scotland and England were men like James King, Patrick Ruthven and Alexander Leslie. King, a Swedish lieutenant-general and Baron, was an Orcadian who served Sweden from 1615 to 1639 and chose the side of King Charles I when he returned to Britain in the latter year. As Lord Eythin he was to command the centre of The King's forces at the Battle of Marston Moor in 1644, at which battle the conduct of Parliamentarian Scots narrowly achieved victory for his Royal master's opponents. Ruthven, who served Sweden from 1608 until 1637, returned to Scotland with a reputation (even among the Swedes) as a heavy drinker to command The King's forces there and was Governor of Edinburgh Castle in 1639. Leslie took the opposite course when he returned after thirty-three years service to Sweden in 1638 as a Swedish field marshal. Laden with gunpowder and ordnance he opposed his King in the name of the Covenant; we shall encounter him and his cause again.

Figures are not available to indicate much about the Scots who followed these and other commanders across the North Sea. We know that the Highlanders were regarded as tough and able to survive on the most basic of nourishment, that they were armed with muskets, long knives and bows and arrows, that they wore bonnets and plaids. We know that in 1626 differing areas of the Highlands were allocated for recruiting to the regiments being raised for service overseas by Lords Reay and Spynie. Because of the relative poverty of the land in the Highlands and their surplus population it seems likely that the majority of Scots who served in the ranks of these mercenary regiments would have been Highlanders.

The seventeenth century is rightly seen as one when both the art and science of war underwent significant changes although, as with most species of change, developments and advances in methods of dealing death and winning battles were gradual rather than sudden. The Thirty Years War provided a proving ground for new types of tactics and for the sophistication of the existing patterns of weapon. The Scottish commanders who returned home at the end of the 1630s came equipped with knowledge of the latest ideas about troop movements, deployment of cavalry, use of artillery and effectiveness of infantry.

The principal battle tactic of the Highland Scot continued to be the wild, terrifying and ungovernable charge, a relic of their *berserk* Viking ancestry, which manifested itself as a shrieking, hairy horde of half-naked savages wielding a variety of cutlery and bent on dismemberment of the opposition.

While Gustavus Adolphus had praised the Highlanders in his armies for their frequently-demonstrated enthusiasm for the termination of life, he developed methods of fighting for his more conventional forces that were equally effective when employed against opponents who had not read the latest drill books. The five or six metre pike was shortened to three or four metres and its users trained in a role of close-support to bodies of musketeers who, in turn, were decreasingly using the old, very heavy musket or *arquebus* which required a support on which to rest the barrel when firing.

The developing manoeuvrability of infantry was accompanied by that of the cavalry which became less of an undisciplined mob of mounted heavyweights and more a lightly-armoured striking force, armed with firearms and swords, which combined rapidity of deployment with a maximum of striking power.

Manoeuvrability was also of great significance to the artillery; light guns were developed on light carriages which were able to move swiftly to the support of other forces. The Scot Sir Alexander Hamilton, encouraged by Gustavus Adolphus, developed guns with a bronze core strengthened by leather hides and iron hoops; they had a short life and were essentially expendable but contributed significantly to developments in artillery tactics by their versatility.

These were the tactics that came back to an unsettled Scotland at the end of the 1630s with men who had known little else than active soldiering for the previous ten or more years. Their weapons combined attributes of the most primitive with examples of the latest technological development.

The Highlanders were, as were – and are – all soldiers, armed according to their rank; their rank in a regiment naturally reflected their place in their clan's social structure.

15

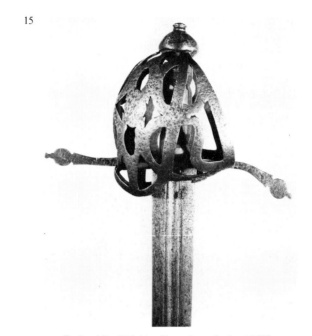

Basket-hilted Highland broadsword, about 1600

13

Musketeer, about 1608.

14

16

Armour of an officer of pikemen, about 1610.

14

Pikeman, about 1608.

Most would have had a *targe*, a disc-shaped wooden shield, covered in leather and decorated with nails with, occasionally, a central spike. Almost all would have been equipped with a knife, or *dirk*, of varying size and quality, generally – but not invariably – single edged and of equal use as an eating as well as a killing implement. Swords were in use fairly far down the ranks by the mid-seventeenth century and although these would principally have been single-handed swords, of varying forms, there are recorded instances of the old two-handed swords being used until almost the end of the century. As we have seen, Highlanders were known also to have been armed with muskets and bows and the richer among them, their officers, would certainly have had pistols too, probably with flintlock ignition systems and by Scottish makers.

The pistol was very much the weapon of the officer among the infantry. Its use by the ordinary soldier was confined to the cavalryman, and a trooper would have a brace of pistols, probably with wheellock ignition systems, in addition to a sword and occasionally a carbine too. Scots cavalry were adept with the lance. Whereas the Highlanders wore little or no protective clothing, the cavalryman would be fairly well protected, against the elements as well as the enemy. A coat of buff leather, doubled in thickness on the skirts, would be worn under a *cuirass* of breast and back-plates; buff leather gauntlets and a buff leather or steel sleeve on his bridle arm, his left, would protect his hands and reduce the likelihood of him losing control of his horse in combat. A metal helmet, of various designs but generally with places or bars over his face, cheeks and neck, or a strengthened broad-brimmed hat, would protect his head, and long boots over heavy breeches would keep him warm and dry. Armed and protected in this manner, the cavalryman had a variety of roles: reconnaissance, skirmishing, shock action, message-bearing, bodyguard duties; he was expected and trained to be the most versatile of soldiers.

Less versatile perhaps, but cheaper to maintain and easier to equip and train was the infantryman. These were divided in roles between those of pikeman and musketeer. The former tended to be larger, stronger men who wore buff leather coats or jerkins under steel breast and back-plates which had *tassets* attached to protect the wearer's groin and thighs; their heads were protected by a steel helmet intended to ward off the downward slash of a cavalry sword. The musketeers wore little body armour in addition to their buff coats or jerkins, but those with any sense (and musketeers tended to be recruited from the less stolid of the infantry) wore steel protective pots under their hats. Although pikemen would still operate in formations designed to advance like ponderous hedgehogs, they would also be increasingly likely to form defensive screens for the musketeers while these reloaded their muskets or changed formation. The musketeers themselves were gradually reduced in number of ranks for most actions so that they could continue to fire volleys by ranks yet retain the destructive capacity to fire massed volleys as required; medical records do not offer evidence of the degree of deafness among seventeenth century musketeers.

17

Cavalry buff coat and steel gorget, about 1630.

Highland *targe*, or shield, about 1630.

These were the types of soldier which characterised the battles of the first half of the seventeenth century. As the century progressed so the pike would fade in importance and the armour of the cavalry diminish as the increased penetrative power of the firearm rendered it redundant. With the exception of the Highlanders, the soldiers of Scotland looked little different from those of the rest of western Europe. The causes for which they fought were much the same too: politics liberally laced with religion.

Such a concoction is an explosive mixture at the best of times and the seventeenth century could not be described as that. In Britain King James VI and I, amply fulfilling his description as the Wisest Fool in Christendom, had died in 1625 leaving his thrones to his eldest surviving son Charles. Charles was an immensely civilised patron of the Arts; he had all the tact of a rhinoceros with a headache, believed rigidly in the Divine Right of Kings at a time that parliaments were beginning to flex their muscles and was contentedly married to a Catholic French Princess when Protestants were feeling at their most threatened. Britain was a powder keg and the fuse was shortest in Scotland.

The National Covenant, drawn up in 1638, reflected the Protestant paranoia that Charles had unleashed by attempting to impose government and doctrines on the Church of Scotland which, seen from a Protestant standpoint, implied a move towards the Church of England, itself felt to be becoming increasingly Romeward bound. As with the causes of the English Civil War though, there was much more to it than religion, important though spiritual matters were to the Scots. Behind The King's actions were perceived incipient despotism and threats to parliamentary government. With a King other than Charles on the throne, matters might have been solved by negotiation: his intractability made it a fighting matter.

A Scots army was mustered, led by Alexander Leslie, equipped with weapons and ordnance brought back by him from the continent and manned by many of the soldiers who had served under him abroad where he had ensured that they had signed the Covenant. One brief battle, at Newburn in 1640, was enough to show Charles that the Scots meant business and there the matter rested, militarily at least. The battle at Newburn is significant to this story for two reasons. Hamilton's leather guns, nicknamed 'Sandy's stoups', were used effectively to soften up the English. The Scots vanguard was led by a man whose title would be written in letters of fire across the Scottish history of the 1640s: James Graham, 5th Earl, and later 1st Marquess, of Montrose.

By 1644 England was two years into its First Civil War and both King and Parliament had approached the Scots for help. At the end of 1643 the Scots Parliament came down on the side of its English equivalent, perceiving that the survival of Presbyterianism depended upon a salutary defeat for the King. 20,000 soldiers were dispatched across the border under the command of Alexander Leslie, created 1st Earl of Leven by the King as a conciliatory gesture in 1641. This move made it necessary for Scots to choose sides; some did so out of principle, some out of opportunism.

18 Montrose attempted an invasion of Scotland through the

Borders in April 1644 but attracted little support and withdrew. He tried again in August, a month after the Scots army had helped its English allies defeat The King's forces at Marston Moor, and was more successful. He was accompanied by 1,000 Irish soldiers led by Sir Alexander MacDonald whose motives were less support of the King than the intention of regaining MacDonald lands from the Campbells under the auspices of loyalty to the Royalist cause. The use of Irish troops as an invasion force was a move guaranteed in the seventeenth century to make the user unpopular in Britain and the sheer professional savagery of these Ulster MacDonalds did nothing to dispel fears about the barbarity of the Irish. At the time, any campaign in the Highlands was likely to succeed by success and, as Montrose and his Irishmen scorched their way across Highland Scotland between September 1644 and August 1645, so their blowtorch was gradually fed by Highlanders eager to share in the spoils. These Highlanders, some MacPhersons, a few Camerons and some men of Glengarry, left Montrose after his victory at Kilsyth to return home, as did such Gordon tenants who had joined him. With depleted forces, weakened still further by the decamping of MacDonald's Irishmen, who had found Campbell throats to cut in Kintyre, Montrose was soundly beaten by the Covenanting forces of David Leslie at Philip-laugh in September 1645. Charles had been defeated finally at Naseby in June 1645 and, realising that his Scots opponents were less personally opposed to him than were his English ones, surrendered to the Scottish Army in May 1646 and ordered Montrose to cease hostilities a month later.

What followed characterised the ambivalence felt by many Scots for The King and his policies. Although opposed to his policies, and deploring his attitudes, the Scots were not opposed to his person. When that person was threatened, as it seemed to be after he had been surrendered to the English parliament, and thence to the English Army, in 1647 the Scots sent an Army into England in The King's support. Ill-prepared and led by the most undistinguished officers that Scotland could provide, it was shattered at Preston, sustaining casualties of ten per cent of its number, in August 1648. The King was executed five months later.

The decapitation of their anointed monarch by the English stunned the Scots and they immediately accepted his son Charles as their King, although only on condition that he bind himself to be a better Presbyterian than his late father. The Swedish connection resurfaced as Patrick Ruthven, now Earl of Forth, and Lords Eythin and Montrose arrived in Stockholm during 1649 to buy arms and ships for an invasion of Scotland in support of King Charles II. Lord Eythin remained to die in Sweden in 1652 but Lords Forth and Montrose embarked in three ships laden, it is recorded, with 3,600 swords, 820 pairs of pistols, harness for 2,000 horses, drums, pikes, standards, shot and gunpowder. Forth joined The King, Montrose landed in Orkney in March 1650 and in April invaded the mainland with a few hundred men. Failing to gain much support he was defeated at Carbisdale, captured and executed in May. A

19

Highland soldiers in the service of the Swedish King Gustavus Adolphus at Stettin (Szczecin) 1631.

20

Highland dirk, about 1670.

King James VI of Scotland and I of England
(1566–1625)

King Charles II (1630–85)

King James III of Scotland and II of England
(1633–1701).

further defeat for the Royalist Scots followed at Dunbar in September when an Army of 23,000 led by David Leslie lost 3,000 killed at the hands of an English Army of 11,000. The defeat was one of David Leslie's few tactical blunders and he made the mistake of making it against one of the few good soldiers who was also to become a competent politician, Oliver Cromwell. Resistance to the Cromwellian forces continued in Scotland and by Scots until the decisive defeat of The King's forces, which included 15,000 Scots, at Worcester in 1651. After Montrose's death the Highlands were more inclined to rally to The King; many MacLeods fell at Worcester and an abortive Royalist rising in the central Highlands in 1654 attracted the support of Camerons, MacKenzies, Frasers and some MacDonalds.

The nature of the government of Britain between 1651 and the return of The King in 1660 was one of savage oppression. Aside from Ireland, which was burnt and massacred into submission relatively quickly, nowhere did this policy manifest itself more firmly than in Scotland. The establishment of the Commonwealth in 1651 incorporated Scotland into Britain and the northern kingdom was ruled from Westminster. The Protectorate, which existed from 1654 until 1660, did the same and treated Highland Scotland as a frontier province. The government of Scotland was military in character and in fact. It was occupied by an army of never less than 10,000 men. Forts were built across the country in strategic locations at Leith, Perth, Ayr, Inverness and Inverlochy where they controlled or monitored tracts of land and sea and could be supplied from either source in case of trouble or attempted blockade. Figures are available

which indicate, in the case of that at Inverlochy, that these forts presented formidable obstacles to potential attackers. Their garrisons were nine or ten companies of infantry; ordnance, twelve cannon of varying calibres – principally *demi-culverins* capable of firing both solid and small shot which would cut bloody swathes through advancing troops; muskets to be *snaphaunces*, an early form of flintlock. The fort at Inverness was massive and designed to intimidate both the Highland capital and its hinterland. These citadels controlled the geography of the country's most troublesome part. The country as a whole was ruled by soldiers. Of the eight Scottish commissioners of the Commonwealth, five were soldiers. Under the Protectorate's Scottish council of state five of the nine members were English soldiers, two were Scots civilians. Until the death of Oliver Cromwell in 1658 Britain was kept firmly under control and Scotland especially so.

The soldiers who garrisoned Scotland during the years of the Commonwealth and Protectorate were those of the New Model Army, created by a Parliamentary Ordinance of 1645. The New Model was an English Army, the first organised, permanent military force to be seen in Britain and the predecessor of the Standing Army created after the Restoration of the Monarchy in 1660. It is clear that the government at Westminster regarded the Army as one of occupation and as uniformly English in character since occasional edicts were issued forbidding English soldiers from marrying Scotswomen, Scots being suspected Royalists. While the English were occupying their country, Scots soldiers were active elsewhere, fighting for a variety of

Lieutenant-General James Graham, 5th Earl and 1st Marquess of Montrose (1612–50)

Lieutenant-General Thomas Dalyell of the Binns (1599–1685)

General Alexander Leslie, 1st Earl of Leven (1580–1661).

masters. There were Scots on both sides at the Battle of the Dunes in 1658; fighting in the Spanish Army in tacit support of King Charles II and in the French forces allied with English New Model regiments. The commander of the Parliamentary forces in Flanders was Sir William Lockhart, a Scot who had fought for both the Dutch Republic and France before the Civil Wars and for both Charles I and Charles II before siding with the Protectorate; he was to change allegiance again at the Restoration. The foreign adventures of the Protectorate coincided conveniently with the need to strip Highland Scotland of its potential warriors and, after the failure of the 1654 Royalist rising, two regiments were ordered to be raised in the Highlands for service abroad in the pay of the Protectorate's allies.

When Charles II returned to Britain as King in 1660 he brought with him Royalist regiments and inherited an Army, based on the New Model, which owed allegiance not to him but to Parliament. Reconciliation of these two potentially-opposing bodies was of prime importance if the security of the throne, and of the government of the country, was to be rapidly established. A minor rebellion of fanatic Protestants against the Restoration revealed the continuing need for a permanent, if reduced, Army and so the gradual paying-off and disbandment of the regiments was stopped in 1661. The basis of the new British Army began with a few regiments of horse and foot in 1661, divided between the English, Scots and Irish Establishments.

In Scotland, the forts built to control the country were gradually dismantled, although some – like that at Inverness – proved so difficult to break-up that parts still remained until the next century. The country was still far from settled since the power and influence of the Covenanters remained, threatening the episcopalian government with increasing disruption. To counter this menace, regiments were raised in Scotland by supporters of the government. A 4th (or Scots) Troop of Life Guards dated from 1661 and survived until 1746; the regiment now known as the Scots Guards was raised in 1662, apparently from the residue of companies originally embodied in 1642 for service in Ireland. Le Régiment de Douglas was brought back briefly from France in 1662 in order to be placed at the head of the newly-constituted British infantry of the line; it still occupies that place under its present title of The Royal Scots (The Royal Regiment). Other bodies of both cavalry and infantry came and went during the 1660s as the domestic and international situations demanded.

A serious outbreak of militant Covenanting in 1666, coupled with renewed war against the Dutch Republic, necessitated an increase in the Scots establishment. After the defeat of the Covenanters at Rullion Green in November 1666, and the signing of peace with the Dutch in 1667, the Scots forces were reduced to their former strength: two troops of Life Guards and the regiment of Foot Guards. The Covenanters' rebellion of 1666 was suppressed with considerable brutality by forces under the command of Lieutenant-General Thomas Dalyell, who wrote of the need to extirpate such rebels by transportation and execution and was popularly credited with their torture.

The later 1660s were marked by several mutinies among Scottish soldiers protesting about not receiving arrears of

27

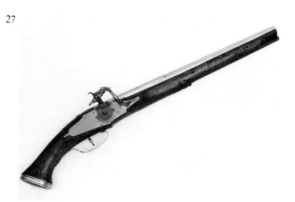

Cavalry wheellock pistol, about 1640.

pay due to them. Three companies of Douglas's (Royal Scots) who had been seconded to the Foot Guards for the Covenanters' rebellion were disbanded in 1667 after refusing to rejoin their unit without first being paid. Seventy men of the Foot Guards deserted in 1670 and prompted a Privy Council enquiry into the soldiers' conditions which found that they were all owed ten months' pay. The civilian population naturally suffered from having unpaid, hungry and armed soldiers in their midst and soldiering, as much as the soldiers themselves, remained unpopular both with potential soldiers and their unwilling paymasters. Both the nation and its government had yet to come to terms with the concept of a permanent Army.

Less permanent and cheaper was the Militia, which had been reorganised in 1661. Eight years later Lord Lauderdale was able to write to The King with an account full of praise for the six Scots militia regiments that he had recently reviewed. His comments chiefly reflected upon their appearance but touched also upon their varying adherence to the Covenant, a factor which he found disturbing.

His fears, and those of others in the government, proved justified when the Covenanters broke into open rebellion again in 1677. The Scots Army was trebled in size during the following year as much to resist a supposed threat from France as to subdue the Covenanters whose home shires in the south-west had seven thousand Highlanders and loyal Lowland Militia billetted on them in order to contain the rebellion. The depredations of the Highland Host, as it was called, did more harm than good and they were withdrawn, laden with loot, in mid-1678. By the time of their withdrawal the threat, such as it was, from France had ended but the Covenanters were resurgent, well-armed and aggressive. Before being finally beaten at Bothwell Bridge by forces led by the Duke of Monmouth in July 1679, the Covenanters had won two victories and occupied Glasgow, giving the government a bad fright. Breakaway forces calling themselves Cameronians, after their leader Richard Cameron, were finally destroyed at Airds Moss in 1680 but

the movement lived on and was to be put to military use by another government a little later on.

Of the regiments raised to subdue the last large-scale rebellion of the Covenanters, those to become The Royal Scots Greys and The Royal Scots Fusiliers survived longest. The Greys, a regiment of Dragoons, were created in 1681 by Thomas Dalyell from troops raised in 1679.

Aside from creating Scotland's only surviving regular cavalry regiment, Dalyell framed Articles of War for the Scots Army in 1667. These ninety-seven articles governed the conduct of officers and men and specified, in no uncertain manner, the savage punishments that the soldier could expect: forty-two identifiable offences carried the death penalty.

The death of Charles II in 1685 brought his Catholic brother James to the throne as James VII of Scotland and II of England. His known religious beliefs and suspected ambitions to reassert the attempted despotism of his father gradually lost him all but his most loyal supporters and culminated in his exile in 1688 when his son-in-law, the Protestant Prince William of the Netherlands, was invited to become King William III by influential members of the English government. In Scotland James's reign gave hope to Catholics, horrified the remaining Covenanters but, at first at least, was generally welcomed; he was, after all, his father's son. His expulsion was very much an English idea and by 1688 he had lost so much support in Scotland that, when the Scots Army of 3,700 men marched to London to back him up against the invasion, there were few loyal forces remaining there to help them prop up his rapidly collapsing administration.

With the flight of James and the accession of William and his consort Mary, the Scots, Irish and English armies ceased to exist as separate entities although retaining their own Establishments. Having spent much of the seventeenth century choosing between King and Covenant and King and Parliament, many Scots, soldiers as well as civilians, were to spend the next sixty years having to choose between monarchs; one based in England, the other over the water.

CHAPTER THREE

LOYAL OR REBELLIOUS?

1688 to 1746

The Army that William III inherited from his dispossessed father-in-law was largely loyal. Defections of officers to Holland had been taking place for some months prior to what its Whig instigators called 'The Glorious Revolution' and after William landed at Torbay, in November 1688, this trickle became a flood. Most soldiers unwilling to join William left with James; these were principally the Catholic officers to whom he had granted commissions and the soldiers who accompanied them. The Army of 1688 was really a refined version of that created from the residue of the New Model Army in 1661. It was refined in terms of its structure and arms; the raw material remained as crude as ever. In size it consisted of the three regiments of Household Cavalry, six regiments of Horse, four of Dragoons, three of Foot Guards and eighteen of line infantry; in addition were the artillery and the supply services. Figures of regimental complements varied considerably but it is reasonable to assess the strength of the cavalry and infantry in 1688 at about 27,000. A further regiment of Horse, two of Dragoons and eight of Foot were raised between the landing at Torbay and the end of 1689 to resist threats to the establishment of the new monarchy.

The armament of the cavalry had changed little since the Civil Wars. The Household Cavalry are known to have been uniformly armed with carbines, in addition to pistols and swords, in 1663; this weapon was extended in general issue to the Horse in 1677. In 1688 the Dragoons were really mounted infantry in character. Armed with flintlock muskets, bayonets and occasionally a *halberd* (a short pike with an axe-head) and a pair of pistols they were the most versatile of soldiers; better armed than the Horse they could move faster than the ordinary Foot.

The infantry had split into the differing, and sometimes specialised, groups that were to begin to characterise this largest part of the Army. Senior were the regiments of Foot Guards, each with two battalions. Their soldiers were armed with flintlock muskets and *bayonets* – the latest things in weapon development and gradually replacing the old matchlock musket and pike combination. Flintlock muskets, or *fusils*, were also the weapons of certain regiments designated as *Fusiliers* whose original role was to guard the artillery train. The fusil, with its inert flint, was safer around stocks of gunpowder than the slow-burning

match of the matchlock musket used by the rest of the infantry. The bulk of British footsoldiers continued to be armed with this matchlock musket although, by 1688, it is likely that at least half of each regiment would have been equipped with flintlocks. The pike was gradually being superseded by the bayonet which, in 1688, was a short double-edged knife with a tapering hilt that was rammed into the muzzle of the musket to convert it into a short pike. Although the pike survived in diminishing numbers for a few years we shall see shortly how the obvious limitations of the plug bayonets were revealed, bloodily, in Scotland. Each infantry battalion consisted of twelve companies with an additional company of *grenadiers*. Grenadiers, usually the tallest and strongest men in the battalion, were specially trained in the use of the *grenade*, an explosive cast iron ball ignited through a wooden fuse, which had first appeared in the Army in the 1670s. Grenadiers, because of their size and the nature of their weapons, were frequently used as assault troops and so, together with Fusiliers, became something of an élite among the infantry. Their headdresses, conical caps rather than the broad-brimmed hats of the ordinary infantrymen, were designed to aid the slinging of their muskets over their shoulders prior to the use of their grenades. As was, and is, the nature of military uniform however, these essentially functional caps rapidly became highly decorative as the honor of wearing one became more eagerly sought.

One of the most obvious ways in which the Army of 1688 differed from its predecessors was that it was a uniformed Army. Scarlet coats had become the recognised uniform of both Horse and Foot in the New Model Army and were retained by most regiments after 1661. The cavalry generally retained the helmet although it was being replaced by the broad-brimmed hat, often with a steelpot reinforcing the crown. Their buff leather coats and other remnants of protective clothing were becoming increasingly redundant in the face of the increased power of musketry but the *cuirass* of breast and back-plate remained, at least for parade and portrait purposes for officers, until the next century. As the function of the pike drained away, so the armoured pikeman was transformed into the red-coated infantryman clad, unless he was a grenadier or fusilier, in a broad-brimmed hat, a long coat with a coloured lining which varied according to his regiment, breeches, hose and shoes. His officers retained, for the next century and a half, a vestige of the armour of the officer of pikemen, the crescent-shaped throat-piece known as a *gorget*. There was little or nothing about the uniform of the Scottish regiments to distinguish them as Scots but it is clear from the few examples of uniform which survive from the period that some use was made of the national flower on gorgets and grenadier caps.

As was said in the previous chapter, the permanent Army was unpopular; with government primarily because it cost money and with people because it was a nuisance, especially when it wasn't paid regularly. James had increased the size of his Army and thereby increased Parliament's opposition to it since, as a body with allegiance sworn to The King, it was a threat as well as an expense. The arrival of William may have lessened the potential threat that the Army posed to the liberties of Parliament but it did nothing to decrease its expense; rather the reverse. William had been invited primarily because he was a Protestant, married to a Protestant Stuart Princess, Mary, and because he was seen as a King whom Parliament could have on their terms. As a Protestant monarch, he represented a threat to the power of Catholic France and her King, Louis XIV, who – rightly – now felt threatened on two fronts, from the Netherlands and from across the Channel. As a supplanter of James, for many people the lawful King – however ghastly he may have

A private of the 25th, or Earl of Rothes's, Regiment of Foot 1742.

Officer's gorget of a Scottish Royal regiment, about 1705.

22

been, William represented a usurper against whom rebellion was justified. In other words, Britain was now to be split by rebellion at home and threatened by war abroad. She had never needed a large permanent Army more and the days of the cheap option were gone for good.

In the three kingdoms that comprised Britain in 1688, the Revolution was received very differently. It was made in England and the English Parliament expected the other two kingdoms to accept it. Ireland didn't and flared into open revolt. Scotland did, but on her own terms and only after a great many self-justifying crises of conscience in the Scots Parliament. James had succeeded in alienating a majority of influential Scots and was deemed to have forfeited his Crown by breaching the unwritten agreement by which he held it; in England he was said to have abdicated. For a few Scots, however, principally those who had done well out of James's reign and hoped to do better, he was the rightful King, from a Scottish dynasty, and could not be deprived of his birthright by the actions of a Parliament, and especially not those of an English Parliament. Memories of the way that the English had treated Charles I, James's father, were revived by his supporters who, utilising the Latin version of his name, *Jacobus*, from the Royal Style and Title, came to be called *Jacobites*. For the next sixty years the Jacobites were to represent the chief threat to the stability of the British monarchy and government. For reasons of economics, geography, tradition and lineage, Scotland represented the power base of this movement and was, as a result, deeply divided. The extent of the division was demonstrated in 1689 by two incidents, a mutiny and a rebellion.

The mutiny occurred in The Royal Regiment of Foot (now The Royal Scots) commanded since 1655 by the Earl of Dumbarton, a Catholic, who had chosen to follow James into exile. He was replaced by the Duke of Schomberg and the regiment was ordered overseas to help confront a threat to the Netherlands from France. Clearly torn in its allegiance between James and William, the regiment changed its mind at its point of embarkation, Ipswich, seized four cannon and turned north. They were caught by a pursuing, and much larger, force in Lincolnshire and surrendered; the ringleaders were imprisoned and then cashiered. The significance of the mutiny of a Scots regiment was only partially lost on Parliament. Although the passing of the Mutiny Act resulted from it, Parliament was still taken unawares by the rebellion which began in April 1689 in Scotland.

It was largely the work of one man. Inspired by the shade of Montrose, that most swashbuckling of Cavaliers, Viscount Dundee, a self-consciously heroic young aristocrat and Colonel of Horse who had gained the favour of Charles II and James by the assiduous pursuit of Covenanters during the previous decade, took upon himself Montrose's mantle as the defender of the Stuart monarchy. By April 1689 the Scots Parliament had voted to accept the sovereignty of William, having protected themselves during the voting procedure by employing a para-military force of rabid Protestants still calling themselves Cameronians. Aware of the potential threat from Dundee and his cavalry, and fearful

29A

A private of the Royal Regiment of North British Dragoons 1742.

29B

A private of 43rd, Lord Sempill's (Highland) Regiment of Foot 1742.

THE SCOTTISH SOLDIER

that he might be successful in drumming up support, they had asked the Earl of Leven to look into the possibility of raising a loyal regiment of Protestants in Edinburgh for the defence of the city. Some accounts of the raising of what ultimately became The King's Own Scottish Borderers in March 1689 indicate that the task was accomplished in a matter of hours.

The Scots Parliament had less cause for concern than they had imagined since Dundee failed to attract the kind of support, both in quality and quantity, for which he had clearly both hoped and expected. When his forces met those of the government, commanded by Hugh Mackay of Scourie, at the northern end of the Pass of Killiecrankie in July 1689, Dundee had less than 2,000 men and Mackay five infantry battalions and two troops of Horse totalling, perhaps, twice that number. Mackay's forces were principally Scots: his own and two other Scots regiments had been withdrawn from the Scots Brigade in the Dutch service and he had Leven's newly-raised Edinburgh Regiment too. Dundee's forces, other than his cavalry, were largely Highlanders: the warriors of petty chieftains from the more impenetrable parts of the Highlands and a ragbag of cattle-thieves, outlaws and other professional villains from the Highland hinterland. As Mackay's forces slowly emerged from the Pass, Dundee's Highlanders were massing, fingering their axes, on the slopes above them. What happened next would dominate the regular British soldier's feelings about Highlanders for the next sixty years. Dundee, seeing his advantage and realising that he had to take it before Mackay could deploy his forces on to more suitable ground, slipped the leash and let free his Highlanders. MacDonalds of Keppoch, of Glencoe and of Clanranald, Camerons, Robertsons of Struan, Macleans of Duart, Stewards of Appin, Macleods of Raasay and MacNeills of Barra; all swept shrieking down the sloping ground towards the horrified apprentices of Edinburgh and the Dutch regiments of Scots who had become acustomed to the carefully-choreographed warfare of Flanders. Of Mackay's forces, the only one to stand firm was the English infantry battalion, Hastings's Regiment, later to become the Somerset Light Infantry and to face a similar onslaught with equal phlegm fifty-seven years later. All the others broke and fled.

While Mackay had been gathering his forces for the march north to find and discourage Dundee, the militancy of the Covenanters had taken on a martial tone, encouraged by the Scots Parliament. The Parliament was aware, as past and future Scots administrators had been and would continue to be, that the best way of controlling a difficult part of the nation was to find people of opposing views and

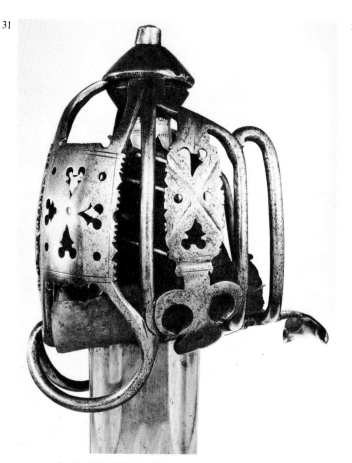

Basket-hilted Highland broadsword, about 1740.

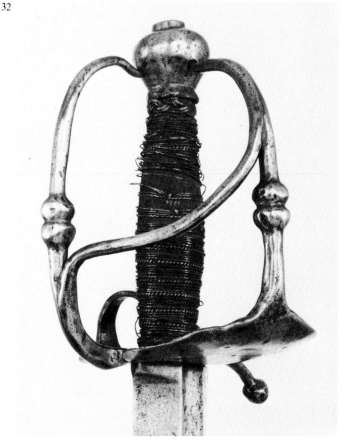

Infantryman's hanger, about 1720.

24

encourage them to change the mind of the opposition. It therefore proposed that the para-military force which had protected them against disturbance by the loyal garrison of Edinburgh Castle, while they were agreeing to the accession of William and Mary, should form a regiment and go Dundee-hunting. After much breast-beating and ruminations upon the sinfulness of soldiers, the attractions of a little Catholic-bashing in the name of the furtherance of the Reformation proved overwhelming and 1,200 Covenanters formed the Earl of Angus's Regiment in May 1689; it survived for nearly three centuries as The Cameronians.

After Killiecrankie, at which Dundee had been killed, the Highlanders marched south, pausing only for a little light looting and pillage, their numbers swelled by the prospect of the sack of Perth. At Dunkeld they found their way barred by Angus's Regiment who fought them to a standstill inflicting estimated casualties of 300 in return for twenty Cameronians killed and fifty wounded. The rebellion was finally brought to an end when those Highlanders who had not made their excuses and left after Dunkeld, or had found easier pickings after Killiecrankie, were caught in the open by Mackay's cavalry at Cromdale on Speyside and routed. In any case, the heart had gone out of it after Dundee's death and the determination of the Cameronians at Dunkeld had effectively finished what had degenerated into

a larger-than-usual Highland raid on the Lowlands.

At Killiecrankie the deficiency of the plug bayonet is said to have been revealed. This had made the infantryman's principal weapon either a musket or a rather inefficient pike: with a head that was inclined to become left in an opponent rather than being withdrawable to spit the next one to come along. What was needed was a bayonet that remained effective while not impeding the prime function of the musket and so the socket or ring bayonet, which fitted around – rather than into – the musket's muzzle, was gradually developed. Although Killiecrankie is thought to have been the catalyst for this development, the French, original developers of the bayonet, had been using socket bayonets for some time before Mackay's soldiers had discovered the deficiency of their plug bayonets in what must, for many of them, have been a fairly terminal fashion. Whatever the truth of the story, French use of the socket bayonet was experienced by Leven's Regiment (King's Own Scottish Borderers) in Flanders during the 1690s. The shock of being fired on by troops with apparently fixed bayonets seems to have been no more than momentary, although it was probably final for some.

The campaigns in Flanders were conducted at the same time as was the pacification of Ireland and Scotland. Ireland was stamped and burnt into submission in a manner

33

Cavalry private's sword, about 1740.

34

Basket-hilted backsword of the type issued to Highland regiments, about 1750.

35

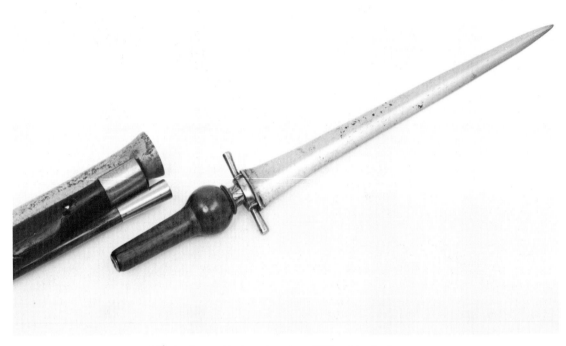

Muzzle of a matchlock musket, about 1670, and its plug bayonet.

reminiscent of Cromwell's campaign there forty years previously but that tortured island was to continue to represent a potential invasion springboard for the government of Britain for several centuries to come. Scotland was quickly recognised both as a focus for Jacobitism at home and as a reservoir of manpower for King William's wars abroad. Accordingly, the country was garrisoned and regiments raised both for the garrisons and for service overseas. In the early 1690s the annual cost of the garrison to William's Exchequer was put at £50,000 and its numbers at three regiments of infantry, scattered about by companies, and seven troops of cavalry. In an effort both to reduce costs and release soldiers for service against the French in Flanders, a negotiated settlement was attempted with certain Highland chiefs. This collapsed when an attempt to make an example of the MacDonalds of Glencoe in 1692 was botched. Soldiers from Hill's Regiment and the Earl of Argyll's Regiment, both of which were disbanded in 1698, attempted a massacre but actually murdered less than forty MacDonalds. It was not much of a massacre by the standards of the time and, since its perpetrators were from regiments raised by a Grant (Hill's) and by a Campbell (Argyll's) it was little more than an extension of the system encouraged by government whereby one group of troublemakers was employed to exterminate another.

Far more effective forms of extermination were being conducted in Flanders however and, between the defeat of the first Jacobite Rebellion in 1689 and the signing of the

Peace of Ryswick in 1697, twenty regiments of infantry and four regiments of Dragoons were raised in Scotland. Most were disbanded during the period or in 1697 and only one of the regiments of Dragoons survives today, now forming part of the Queen's Own Hussars. In addition to these regiments proper, independent companies of Highlanders continued to be raised, as and when required, to police the parts of the Highlands inaccessible to conventional troops or at a distance from one of the garrisons. By offering bribes of money or influence, by sending her young men abroad and by keeping a tight rein on those who remained, Scotland was kept relatively peaceful. Even episodes such as the Glencoe incident, a political gift to Jacobite propagandists which amply demonstrated the delicacy with which William's government pursued their Scottish policy, failed markedly to produce an active reaction except in the very short term.

The wars waged against France by William and, following his death in 1702, by his sister-in-law Queen Anne, occupied the years 1689 to 1713, with an uneasy peace between 1697 and 1701. These were the wars which provided the baptism of fire for the British Army, which laid the foundations of the British Empire, which made the name of John Churchill, Duke of Marlborough, famous, and which provided some of the earliest battle honours still borne on the Colours of the oldest British regiments. Little is known about the parts played in these wars by the short-lived Scottish regiments and what is known about the roles of the six regiments which have survived until the twentieth

36

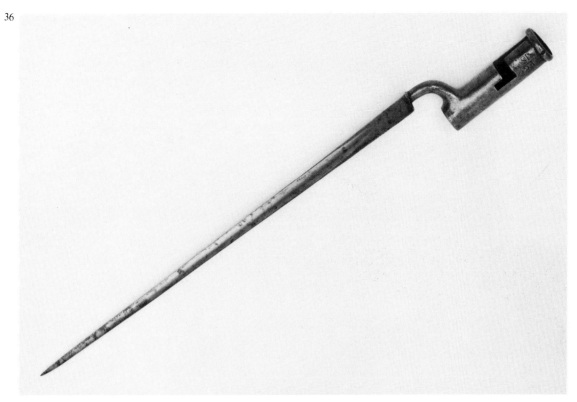

A British socket bayonet of about 1780.

century necessarily concentrates on the view from the commissioned ranks. We know next to nothing about the composition of the Scottish regiments of these wars and less about the men that they contained. It is certain that not all were Scots; it is equally certain that Scots served in non-Scottish regiments. A proportion would have been Highlanders, but not discernible as such when dressed in uniform – probably the only clothes they would possess; none would have been Catholics. All would be above a minimum height, few would be literate. Many would be enlisted while drunk or have the edges of their doubts blunted with alcohol; some would enlist as an alternative to gaol, or starvation, or domestic responsibilities. They would often be despised by their countrymen, cheated by their non-commissioned officers and ignored or patronised by their officers. These officers would mainly have gained their commissions by buying them, many of them feeling that their position in Society gave them the right to command men and to expect the deference that their social position demanded. The commands for which they competed led them and their soldiers into wars bloodier than anyone at the time can have known, yet composed of campaigns in which disease killed more men than musket balls.

Each of the Scottish regiments has pages in its regimental history which deal with the part played by the regiment in Marlborough's wars. It is in the nature of such publications that success is reported more often than defeat, that details of the numbers of officers killed or wounded are more

regularly recorded than similar figures about other ranks. There is no reason to suppose that the Scottish regiments were braver, or more daring, than their English, Irish or Welsh counterparts, yet each played a conspicuous part in the sieges and battles that are now, for most people, no more than names on regimental Colours: Namur, Blenheim, Ramillies, Oudenarde, Malplaquet. One of the differences between the Scots regiments and the others, however, was that the latter were decreasingly called upon to fight their own countrymen.

The Jacobite menace had not decreased with the death of James VII and II in 1701. His son James, known eventually – once he too had a son – as the Old Pretender, became James VIII and III in exile and provided a figurehead for those Scots and few English who believed that he represented a type of greener grass on the other side of the Channel. The Act of Union of 1707 which joined Scotland and England (with all the subtlety of a shotgun wedding) provoked howls of outrage from those in Scotland who had either not been bribed to accept it or were insufficiently short-sighted to see the few economic advantages that the Act presented. There are still those who believe that it was less an Act of Union than one of rape but, whatever the case, it sparked off another Jacobite rebellion in a wholly predictable manner as, suddenly, the Jacobite cause was able to be associated with Scots nationalism and not just tainted with pro-French treason. That fact aside, the French were only too happy to help create confusion in Britain in

27

37   38   39

Queen Anne (1665–1714)   Prince James Francis Edward Stuart, Prince of Wales and King James VIII and III in exile, "The Old Pretender" (1688–1766).   King George I (1660–1727)

order to distract Marlborough who had just thrashed them at Ramillies and so, in 1708, a small expedition set sail. A few lairds supported the attempt and there was much strapping on of broadswords, martial striding about and drinking of loyal toasts but none of the great families moved when James and his followers arrived off the Fife coast in a couple of French ships. Much to James's chagrin, his little flotilla ran away at the sight of a Royal Naval squadron appearing over the horizon and so the Rebellion of 1708 never really materialised. In view of the state of Scotland's defences, neglected considerably in order that the war in Flanders and Spain might be actively pursued, it was as well for Queen Anne's government that James had not landed since he would not have been opposed and could have been something of a nuisance.

Despite trying really hard, Queen Anne had not produced an heir by the time of the Act of Union and so it was arranged that the succession to the thrones of England and Scotland would pass, on Anne's death, to the Elector George of Hanover. George, while he had a blood claim to the thrones that was far less direct than that of the exiled James, was a safe Protestant and enemy of the French. In 1714 Anne died and the Elector became King George I.

A detailed examination of the causes of the inevitable Jacobite Rebellion which followed the accession of George I is outside the compass of this book; it has also been done better elsewhere. Led by the Earl of Mar, for reasons of the purest self-interest, the Rebellion attracted a greater degree of support in Scotland than had earlier Rebellions. So large

was Mar's Army that the Duke of Argyll, Commander in Chief of The King's Army in Scotland, seriously doubted the capacity of his meagre forces to contain them and prevent them from storming south to link up with a rebellion in northern England. The opposing forces met only once seriously in Scotland.

This meeting was on the field of Sheriffmuir, a mile or so north-east of Dunblane and six or seven miles away from the strategic crossing-point of Scotland defended by the Castle of Stirling. Sheriffmuir was, and is, rolling moorland intersected by the Allan Water and other minor burns and lying close to the swelling curves of the Ochil Hills. It was a field on which only a truly incompetent commander could lose a battle, especially if his forces outnumbered those of his enemies by at least four to one. Fortunately for the government of George I, Mar was truly incompetent. At the end of the day's fighting, in November 1715, both armies had won a little and lost a little. Argyll, expecting to be annihilated by weight of numbers, regrouped in the lull presented to him by Mar's unnecessary, but characteristic, withdrawal from the field. The Scots regiments later known as The Royal Scots Fusiliers and The King's Own Scottish Borderers fought on the government side, the Fusiliers losing 91 men killed and 27 wounded out of total government casualties of 377 killed and 153 wounded. The Borderers lost an officer after the battle: hearing that James had landed in Scotland, Captain The Hon. Arthur Elphinstone deserted to join him. Other formerly loyal officers in Scottish regiments had made this decision before Sheriff-

40   41   42

John, 6th Earl of Mar (1675–1732)   Field Marshal John, 2nd Duke of Argyll   Lord George Murray (1700–60)
                                            (1678–1743).

muir; Lord George Murray – to become one of the most competent of Jacobite commanders – having resigned his commission in The Royal Scots in order to serve the exiled Stuarts. The Cameronians, whose loyalty to the cause of Protestant government was less in doubt, had sustained more than 50% of the total casualties incurred in the recapture of Preston from English Jacobites on the day after Mar had lost the battle of Sheriffmuir.

Although characterised by defeat, the potential for success presented by the 1715 Jacobite Rebellion was not lost on the British government. It had seen how the pathetic loyal forces garrisoning the ramshackle Highland strong-points had either been swept aside or, more significantly perhaps, pointedly ignored by the Highlanders as they had poured past to join Mar in the south. Another scare in 1719 culminated in the Battle of Glenshiel between a handful of Jacobites, a few shivering Spanish soldiers and an over-whelming government force who beat and captured the Spaniards and chased the Highlanders back into the heather. Clearly something had to be done about this area of petty monarchs, treason and general nuisance.

In 1717 the Independent Companies of Highlanders, then three in number, were disbanded. This rural local police force had been of no use in the '15 Rebellion, and was probably suspected of treason anyway (even if its position as being of the locality yet being expected to wear the Govern-ment's uniform had not made its position invidious). It was felt that files of Redcoats could manage to exert The King's Writ in the Highlands as adequately as ever without the help of bilingual savages whose motives were, at best, uncertain. The limits of this – very Westminster civilian – view were demonstrated in 1719 and loudly proclaimed by any soldier with local Scottish experience whenever he got the chance. Even the Disarming Act passed after the 1715 Rebellion was a ludicrous failure since it could not be enforced upon High-land society by lumpish Redcoats, English or Lowland Scots, who were more at sea north and west of the Tay than they were in Flanders. Clearly the Independent Companies had to be revived, an inevitable move recommended by General George Wade, an Irish Protestant, after being sent north in 1724 by The King to investigate remedies for the apparently unquenchable lawlessness of the Highlands.

Wade's estimate of the fighting potential of the Highlands in 1724 was 27,000 men, of which at most 10,000 might just about, on a good day, be considered loyal to George I. He recommended that six Independent Companies be raised, totalling about 300 men and officered by carefully-chosen – and apparently loyal – individuals. When the Companies were raised in 1725 the officers were three Campbells, a Munro, a Grant and the man who had suggested the whole idea to George I, Simon Fraser, Lord Lovat. Lovat was an amoral, evil scoundrel whose biography must be read elsewhere but he survived as a captain in the Independent Companies until 1739 when four more companies were added and the whole regimented to form the Earl of Crawford's Regiment of Foot in the Highlands. The regi-ment is now known as The Black Watch (Royal Highland Regiment). Its original soubriquet, now part of its title,

43

44

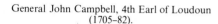

45

General John Campbell, 4th Earl of Loudoun (1705–82).

The popular view of a Highland soldier: a piper of the 43rd, or Lord Sempill's, (Highland) Regiment of Foot about 1743.

A private of the 43rd, or Lord Sempill's (Highland) Regiment of Foot 1742.

indicated the dark colour of its tartan plaid and its function – the Watch being an eighteenth century term for a police force.

In addition to creating Britain's oldest surviving Highland regiment, Wade built roads, barracks and forts across Scotland. Some of the barracks still survive, many of the roads are now buried under asphalt and tarmacadam. It would be incorrect to credit Wade with the introduction of Highlanders into the Army, however, since the men from the hills had been joining British regiments for some time prior to the creation of Lord Crawford's Highlanders. On becoming British soldiers, though, they had discarded the garb worn at home and adopted the scarlet coat, waistcoat and breeches and the long white gaiters of the Redcoat. Unique about Crawford's Highlanders was the fact that they were the first regiment to be kilted, to wear a standardised version of the dress worn at home.

Not that these Highlanders wore kilts as we understand them today: essentially a skirt pleated at the back and wrapped around to form a double layer at the front. They wore *plaids*: the name of the garment rather than a description of its pattern. The plaid, variously known now as the belted or large plaid to distinguish it from later versions, was essentially a large blanket of homespun wool. Ideally, it would be as long as its owner was tall and several times as wide as his, or her, shoulders. After dressing in his shirt and any other desired undergarments, the Highlander would lay upon his plaid, which he had spread upon the ground, bunched in the middle and under which he had

placed his belt, wrap the plaid around him and fasten the belt around his waist. On standing, the plaid would naturally fall into a double wrap-around skirt; the top layer would generally be gathered, fastened with a pin at one shoulder and form a wrap-around shawl if required. The men of the Independent Companies wore plaids standardised at some point early in the eighteenth century and issued to them by the Government; woven in black, dark blue and dark green, and probably not to a standard pattern, a version of this Government tartan is still worn by The Black Watch.

In addition to their plaids, the Highland soldiers wore short waistcoats and coats of standard scarlet, blue bonnets and red and white checked hose above buckled black brogues of cow-hide. Each man was a walking arsenal: musket and socket bayonet, basket-hilted broadsword of the type already known as a *claymore* (an anglicisation of the Gaelic *claidheamh mor*: great sword), a dirk and, often, a pair of pistols. The more senior his rank, the better quality the weapons. Each man had a cartridge pouch and a *sporran*. Sergeants carried halberds instead of muskets, officers were armed with fusils.

Rank in Crawford's Highlanders conveyed little to its possessors since the ranks of this regiment were not filled with Society's refuse, as they often were elsewhere in the Army. At their first muster at Aberfeldy in 1740 many of the private soldiers brought their servants with them to carry their weapons and accoutrements. These private soldiers were the sons of what in Highland Society counted for

30

minor gentlemen and thought it an honour to serve The King rather than an alternative to the prison bulk or the gutter. They were rapidly to be disabused of the notion held by many of them that service in a King's regiment was no different to that in an Independent Company of the Watch. The King's regiments were subject to military discipline, liable for service abroad and officered by men social light years from those in the ranks.

The Highland regiment intrigued The King. George II, who had succeeded his father in 1727, tipped two Highland privates a guinea each after they had been brought to London for him to see and had demonstrated cuts with their broadswords. It was a generous and well-meant gesture and most private soldiers would have instantly converted the gold into days of studied inebriation. The Highlanders, who felt themselves to be at least as good as any of The King's fawning noble courtiers, promptly gave the money to a Royal porter on their way out.

Not everyone showed The King's enthusiasm for the Highlanders; some, remembering how useless the Watch had been during the 1715 Rebellion and, indeed, how many of its members had followed their chiefs into the ranks of the rebels, proposed that the regiment be be sent abroad as quickly as possible to lessen the number of potential rebels in the Highlands. Others were contemptuous of these outlandlishly-dressed savages who spoke little or no English yet behaved with the arrogance of gentlemen.

In 1742 the regiment was ordered south and in 1743 crossed the border, assured by its officers that it was to be reviewed by The King. Such assurance became less and less convincing and the few men who had deserted at once on hearing that they were to leave the Highlands were joined by an increasing number of their comrades as Scotland became further away and the inevitable killing ground of Flanders approached. Matters were made worse when some Highlanders were told by some Royal Scots that their destination was the Caribbean and not the Low Countries. The Royals had returned from a campaign in the West Indies in 1742, having suffered 90% casualties – all from disease, and their tales of horror would have conveyed a lot to those Highlanders familiar with the Caribbean only as a place to which their seditious countrymen were transported and from which they rarely returned. At length, believing that their officers had broken faith with them and thus forfeited the right to be obeyed – by the tenets that ordered Highland society, a part of the regiment mutinied. They had, they believed, enlisted to serve at home. It was not that they feared death by musket balls or grape-shot in Flanders, although they did – they admitted – fear a shivering, vomiting death in the Caribbean, it was that they had been lied to, traduced and suborned and they decided, simply, to go home. In an Army where lying to recruits was expected and traducement an art form, a reaction of such naïveté provoked outraged bewilderment rapidly followed by spluttering anger at the Highlanders' ingratitude. The mutiny amply demonstrated the size of the gulf that still existed between Highland Scotland and the rest of Britain. It never stood a chance of course and, after the 100 or so mutineers

had been halted, persuaded to surrender and imprisoned in the Tower, three were shot (by soldiers of the Scots Guards) and the remainder transported overseas to regiments anxious for recruits. Their regiment embarked for Flanders without them and was blooded, expensively, at Fontenoy in 1745 before being ordered back later in the year when the last Jacobite Rebellion took place.

During the 1720s and '30s the Lowland Scottish regiments had been occupied on the continent of Europe, in the West Indies, in Ireland and in Scotland as combatant or garrison forces for a government that was beginning, grudgingly, to accept the existence of a permanent army as its necessary arm in policing the increasing areas of its responsibility. The Scots Greys, Scots Guards and Royal Scots Fusiliers fought at Dettingen in 1743, the last battle when a British King commanded his soldiers in person, and they, together with The Royal Scots and King's Own Scottish Borderers suffered heavy casualties at Fontenoy in 1745 when the Army in Flanders was commanded for the first time by The King's son, William, Duke of Cumberland. Cumberland gained valuable lessons in the effect of sustained volley-firing at Fontenoy that he was shortly to employ less expensively, in terms of the lives of his own soldiers, in Britain.

His father, The King, was deeply interested in his Army, although it is debatable how much the Royal concern was limited to the immaculacy of its appearance. Throughout his reign, George had kept a close eye, amounting to interference, on the dress of the Army and, in the absence of much in the way of surviving material from the 1740s, students of military uniform have reason to thank this King for commissioning the drawings and paintings of his soldiers that were produced in the 1740s.

Little, unfortunately, was done to improve the lot of the soldier during the same period. He was paid a minimum of six pence (2½p) per day, most of which was stopped out of his pay to reimburse his Colonel for the cost of his uniform and his basic food, for which the Colonel of each regiment remained responsible, to the extent that his regiment was virtually his own property. The average private soldier in a line infantry regiment did well if he managed to retain one penny (½p) per day and, from this, he had to supplement his diet. He would be at least five feet five inches tall – although this would diminish in a ratio dependent upon Government's desperation for recruits – and subject to a system of savage discipline which utilized either corporal or capital punishment to deter him from breaking the many rules that governed his existence. Enlisted for the usual variety of reasons and bribed by a bounty on enlistment of three of four pounds, he might equally well be cudgelled by a press-gang or spared the lingering or revolting death prescribed by civil courts of law for most offences by agreeing to be a soldier. Once enlisted he would be dressed in a scarlet wool coat with heavy lapels, deep cuffs and long skirts, scarlet waistcoat and breeches, long white canvas gaiters called *spatterdashes*, thin-soled shoes of little practical use and a black felt three-cornered hat. Grenadiers still wore their conical caps, now tall and resembling the *mitre* of a bishop

The ruins of Ruthven Barracks, Kingussie, Inverness-shire. Built in 1720, destroyed in 1746.

with a variety of regimental and Royal devices embroidered on the front. Cavalry uniforms varied little from those of the infantry, in essentials, except that leather breeches and long heavy boots clad the troopers' legs.

The infantryman's arms had changed little since the beginning of the century. His principal weapon was still the musket, but by the 1740s all soldiers had flintlocks, each with a 46 inch barrel firing a lead ball three-quarters of an inch in diameter and weighing over an ounce. Available for fixing around its muzzle was a fluted steel bayonet sixteen inches long; this usually hung by his side together with a short curved sword called a *hanger*. Only Highlanders were better armed and by the 1740s their native weapons, broadsword and steel pistols, were cheap things knocked together in the shops of Birmingham. Cavalry weapons remained the pistols, carbine and sword, the latter a single-edged straight yard of steel with a basket-hilt which, if wielded with a strong arm from the height provided by horseback, was capable of inflicting disabling wounds on dismounted troops.

These were the soldiers who were withdrawn from conventional wars on the continent of Europe to confront the menace of Jacobitism renewed when its figurehead, Prince Charles Edward Stuart, landed in Scotland in July 1745.

By the time that those Scottish regiments who were to be involved in the suppression of this dying flourish of the Jacobite cause arrived in Britain, it was almost all over. After initial successes had carried the Jacobite Army as far south as Derby, the obvious lack of active support from the majority of English Jacobites and a similar lack of encouragement from France had combined with the rapid build-up of forces under Cumberland to necessitate a strategic withdrawal to Scotland. There, increasingly discouraged, and with many of his supporters finding excuses to return home as the discouragement became contagious, Charles Edward fought his way back to the North winning a brief but significant victory at Falkirk on the way. Falkirk was significant for two reasons: it was won by the last successful Highland charge and that charge was successfully resisted by an English regiment who were to benefit from that experience later in the year. The Jacobite forces retreated through central Scotland, via the Pass of Drumochter leaving Cairn Gorm on their right as, pausing to deflate the confidence of the commander of the tiny garrison in Ruthven Barracks, they approached Inverness and nemesis. Cumberland took the coastal route around the Grampian mountains, paused at Nairn and advanced to meet his cousin on Drummossie Moor south of Culloden House.

Drawn up in two lines, about 100 yards apart at their closest, the two Armies ended at Culloden the last civil war in Scotland. Like all Jacobite rebellions it had divided families; sometimes for reasons of conscience, sometimes for political expediency. Lord George Murray, formerly an officer in The Royal Scots, now faced his old regiment as its men loaded their muskets and fixed their bayonets. Captains James and John Chisholm, sons of The Chisholm, must have looked across the moor for their brother Roderick who led his father's clansmen on that day against his brothers in The Royal Scots. Campbell's Regiment of Scots Fusiliers and Sempill's Regiment of Scottish Borderers had little in common with the ragged, shrieking mob that rushed down upon them. The reminiscences of Edward Linn, a private in Campbell's Fusiliers, indicate little regret but rather considerable irritation at having to be bothered with such a rabble. The capture of Lord Balmerino who, thirty years before – when he was the Hon. Arthur Elphinstone, had deserted his regiment to join Charles Edward's father, may have given a little satisfaction to those in Sempill's Borderers who were concerned about their regiment's reputation.

The vain Highland charge into a hail of canister shot and musket balls sent a way of life into history. Its final eradication owed a little to a few, frankly sadistic, Scottish soldiers, rather more to Government policy and the beginnings of Imperialism, and a great deal to hard economic facts of life that changed the attitudes and characters in control of life in the Highlands. As we shall see, the suicide charge at Culloden contributed enormously to the story of the Scottish soldier.

The great bombard *Mons Meg*, made at Mons in 1449 and given to King
James II of Scotland in 1457. Her bore is 18 inches (46cm)

Colonel Patrick Ruthven (1573–1651) as a soldier of Sweden 1623.
He later became general in the Army of King Charles I, governor of
Edinburgh Castle and was created Earl of Forth.

Captain James King (1589–1652) as a soldier of Sweden 1623. He
later became lieutenant-general in the Army of King Charles I and
was created Lord Eythin.

I

Embroidered mitre cap of a Grenadier officer in a Scottish infantry regiment, about 1690. The front bears the joint cyphers of King William and Queen Mary between two thistles. The earliest example of military headdress known to survive in Britain.

II

HRH The Prince William Augustus, Duke of
Cumberland (1721–65)

Prince Charles Edward Stuart, Prince Regent,
'The Young Pretender' (1720–88)

The Battle of Culloden 1746; Highlanders attacking 4th, or Barrell's, Regiment of Foot.

An aerial view of Fort George, Ardersier, Inverness-shire, built after the last Jacobite rebellion.

Lieutenant-General Archibald Montgomerie, 11th Earl of Eglinton (1726–96) in the uniform of 77th (Montgomerie's Highlanders) which he raised in 1757.

Lieutenant-General the Rt. Hon. Sir John Sinclair of Ulbster Bart, as Commander of the Rothesay and Caithness Fencibles, about 1794.

IV

CHAPTER FOUR

A MARTIAL RACE

1746 to 1800

The slaughter at Culloden did not materially affect the fighting potential of the clans. Although the canister shot, musket balls, stabbing bayonets and slashing cavalry swords of the government forces at Culloden accounted for an estimated 1,700 Highlanders, the same number survived the battle – in varying degrees of health – and retreated into the Highlands in various semblances of order. Some ran away; some regrouped and marched off, protected from being cut down by Cumberland's Dragoons by the disciplined volley-firing retreat of the French regulars in the Young Pretender's army. Their leaders though, or those with any sense – like Lord George Murray, realised that it was all over.

It had, of course, been all over before it had begun and many chiefs who joined the young man soon to be romanticised as Bonnie Prince Charlie realised that the whole affair was a lost cause when he arrived in July 1745 with no French gold and no French soldiers. Like so many of his Stuart forebears, Charles Edward's hearing was decidedly selective – he heard what he wanted to hear – and so he had ignored the oft-repeated advice of many of his putative supporters in the Highlands that, without gold and soldiers, the idea of a Rebellion simply wasn't on. Highland society and the economic facts of Highland life were changing and Scotland as a whole had not the reason to support the Rebellion of 1745 that it had to support that of 1715. The '45 was a minority movement not a national crusade. That it was as successful as it was owed much to the pusillanimity of the British government in denuding the Highlands of proper garrisons and Britain as a whole of regular troops in the cause of foreign adventures. Once the regulars returned in quantity it was all up with the rebels.

Because the '45 had attracted such a small degree of support among the Highland chiefs, support restricted largely to the smaller clans or sections of clans, there were large numbers who had remained loyal. Probably the most considerable portion of these loyal Highlanders had been those for whom antipathy to the Stuart cause had been almost traditional: the Campbells, headed by the Duke of Argyll. The regimenting of The Black Watch in 1739 and its removal from Scotland three years later would have left the country without its Highland police force had not other, frequently privately-organised, Watches been formed.

Although these were often organised by groups of chiefs or lairds who were primarily loyal to the Westminster government, there were instances when, influenced by less scrupulous individuals – like Lord Lovat, these private police forces operated more like protection rackets than guardians of The King's Peace. It was in an effort to regulate the operations of these private Watches, as well as to seduce dilatory chiefs away from the temptations of Jacobitism, that the government called upon a Campbell, John Campbell, Lord Loudoun, to raise a Highland regiment in 1745. Coincidentally, it sprang into existence a mere four months before the Young Pretender landed.

Loudoun's Regiment had another function too, one which was recognised before it – and the others – became swamped by the rekindling of the Jacobite cause. Several Highland gentlemen held active commissions in Scots regiments of the French Army and, as generations of their ancestors had done, used the influence that they had in their own lands to recruit men there for the service of the King of France. While such practices might have done in the past they would not do when France was at war with Britain and the government in London was seeking to extend its credibility throughout the country. Chief among the offenders was Alasdair MacDonnell, Younger of Glengarry. Along with his commission as a Captain in Loudoun's Regiment, Ewan MacPherson, Younger of Cluny, was issued with instructions to find young Glengarry and change his mind for him. Readers may imagine Cluny's confusion when, a month or so after receiving both his captaincy and his legalised opportunity to extend MacPherson territory, he was summoned by Charles Edward Stuart to join the growing Jacobite forces massing in the north-west. Such personal crises of conscience were common during the '45 but not all had the ill-luck of poor Cluny: declaring for the government, he was captured, made an offer he couldn't refuse and given a colonelcy in the Jacobite Army. His action made him a traitor as well as a colonel and he spent nine years on the run after Culloden, a battle in which he arrived too late to participate. The Clan Campbell, representing the largest confederation of Highland interests and securely based in Argyll, did not have the problems of the smaller chiefs; their very size made them invulnerable to seduction. So, while Loudoun's Regiment skilfully avoided

47

A guard and officers of the 25th Regiment of Foot in Minorca 1769. The four soldiers on the left are grenadiers of the 3rd, 11th, 13th and 67th Regiments of Foot.

anything resembling a pitched battle during the '45, and merely raided where it could, a few hastily-raised Campbell levies, which some writers have glorified with the title of Militia, contrived to be present at Culloden where chances were taken to settle a few old scores.

While continuing traditional practices, like beating up for recruits for foreign armies, Highland chiefs were gradually coming to terms with the new Royal dynasty. The failure of the rebellion, the brutal pacification of the Highlands which followed it and the rapid and enforced transition from much that was medieval to much that was modern completed and hastened the process. In the long term, as we shall see in this chapter, the changes in Highland society eventually produced an icon beloved of the Scottish Tourist Board and anyone else armed with a contract to promote anything Scottish: the Highland soldier.

All this was in the future though as the Redcoats swept through the villages and glens of the Highlands in a reign of terror aimed at stamping out the will to rebel. The Lowland Scottish regiments who had shot down their countrymen at Culloden had little to do with the cultural and physical genocide which followed the battle; less because their loyalty was suspected than because another war existed to require their services elsewhere. France continued to be an active enemy during the War of the Austrian Succession, until peace was signed in 1748, and it was her inability or unwillingness actively to aid the Jacobite cause, as much as the depredations of the government forces in the Highlands,

which finally killed thoughts of another rising.

The Peace of Aix-la-Chapelle in 1748 was, in reality, merely a truce. Although active war was not to break out in Europe for eight years following it, Britain and France locked horns abroad in trials of strength which, in their use of native peoples to do their fighting, were essentially similar. The vast areas affected, where French and British influences had rubbed each other raw to an increasing extent by the 1750s, were India and North America.

English merchants had been trading with accessible parts of the sub-continent since the beginning of the seventeenth century, the East India Company having been given a charter by Elizabeth I in 1600, and English soldiers appeared there, to serve the Company's interests, in 1644. Thus began the Army of the East India Company, in which so many Scots were eventually to serve. Beginning with a core of European regiments (white officers and men), the Company soon began recruiting native regiments (white officers and, at first, non-commissioned officers and native soldiers). For large campaigns, especially ones against the French until their expulsion in 1761, Royal troops would be sent to India to fight alongside the Company's regiments. As India became less of a trading post, and more a part of the burgeoning Empire, so the movement of Royal troops to India would increase. Between 1749 and 1755, years ostensibly of peace in Europe, Britain and France clashed repeatedly in India and, in the latter year, the conflict winding down temporarily in the East, was extended to North America.

Soldiers of the 25th Regiment of Foot at drill, led by a fifer and the drum-major, about 1768.

Scottish soldiers would have been seen in North America since the early seventeenth century, when the colony of Nova Scotia was founded. By the early years of the eighteenth century there were Highland settlers in the Carolinas and Highland emigrants were shipped to Georgia during the 1730s and '40s to help establish and protect that new colony. Scots, predominantly Highland in origin, were established in other outposts as far apart as Florida and Upper New York State by the 1730s too, and after the '45 emigration sharply increased. As in India, both British and French interests in North America grew at the same time, although the French seem to have been more interested in trade than settlement, and so a clash was inevitable. Throughout 1754 tension intensified, skirmishes multiplied and the war began.

The early years of the campaign were ones of embarrassment and shock for the British and indifference turning to panic for the colonists as their forces were out-fought by the French and their forces were out-fought by the French and their Indian allies. With the notable exception of that of Virginia, perhaps because it was commanded by one George Washington, the Provincial militia units were useless. Grudgingly funded by their Assemblies, they were ill-equipped and under-motivated. The British regular regiments reacted to the Indians in much the same way as their peers had reacted to the Highlanders at the battles of Prestonpans and Falkirk; terrified by stories of savagery, they became easily demoralised and often ran away. It was not an encouraging start to what was to become a significant

campaign, both for the history of North America and for the development of the soldiers of Scotland.

When war in Europe was resumed in 1756 it caught the British government with its nether garments in the customary lowered position. After the peace of 1748 Parliament had fallen with its usual glee upon the Army and had disbanded regiments in large quantities in a frenzy of money-saving. During the war, which was to be known as the Seven Years War in Britain and the French and Indian War in America, Britain was required to fight France on three fronts: Europe, India and North America including the Caribbean. It was, in terms of its global coverage, a world war.

The chapter of disasters in America during 1755 had given the government a scare though, and eleven more line infantry regiments were raised during the early months of 1756. By this time the practice was becoming standard of referring to a regiment by a number rather than by the name of whoever happened to be its Colonel, but the two usages remained, frequently employed together, for the next decade. In addition to the augmentation of the infantry, each of the regiments of Dragoons had a light troop added to it. These light troops of Dragoons, who wore suitably distinguishing headdresses, were intended as mounted skirmishers and trained in a far more versatile use of their lighter horses and equipment than were their more conventional comrades who had gradually lost the traditional role of Dragoons as mounted infantry. Experience of a completely new type of warfare in America was to lead quickly to the use of light companies of infantry too but, for the moment, that role of rapidly moving skirmishers operating outside the drill-book movements of the conventional infantry, was confined to Highlanders. The conventional infantry retained their uses though, primarily in the European theatre of operations. This was demonstrated at the Battle of Minden in 1759 when a small number of British infantry regiments, including the 25th (now King's Own Scottish Borderers) marched steadily through an opposing artillery barrage, shattered several large-scale French cavalry charges with rigidly-disciplined musketry and routed a body of opposing infantry too. Their losses were colossal.

By 1759 the war was joined in earnest on all three fronts. The 42nd (Black Watch), augmented by a second battalion raised in 1756, had been murderously treated at the assault on Fort Ticonderoga in 1758, losing 314 killed and 333 wounded in a day's dogged fighting. A supplementary battalion was mustered in Perth in a matter of weeks later in the year. The 2nd battalion of the 1st Foot (Royal Scots) was also involved in America, first in the capture of Louisbourg and then in operations against Cherokee Indians in South Carolina. In this latter action they were accompanied by a regiment of Highlanders which had been raised in 1757 by Archibald Montgomerie and which was known as Montgomerie's Highlanders, or the 1st Highland Battalion, or the 62nd Foot or the 77th Foot, such was the confusing frequency with which regiments could be renamed or renumbered at the time. Apart from its variety of aliases, Montgomerie's had the distinction of being the first Highland regiment of a new generation of such regiments.

These regiments were necessitated not only by the increase in the traditional theatres of operations but also because it was rapidly realised that conventional forces were of little use in the type of war being fought in America. Having learnt by the example of the 42nd Foot how useful Highlanders could be once they had been (comparatively) tamed; having discovered by bitter experience that the Provincial militia units in America were either unwilling or unable, in the main, to provide viable fighting units and having determined, by a survey in the 1750s, that Highland Scotland contained about 12,000 young men, all potential soldiers, the government at Westminster set about utilising these Scottish savages to fight American ones. In this endeavour they were eagerly assisted by Scottish landowners wanting to demonstrate their loyalty to The King and, by so going, perhaps to regain estates forfeited after the '45. In raising their regiments they were assisted by the fact that the Disarming Act of 1747 had proscribed the wearing of Highland dress and carrying of weapons by anyone other than those in the service of The King.

Prominent among those former Jacobites was Simon Fraser, Master of Lovat, son of that wicked old schemer Lord Lovat whose sins had finally found him out and for which he had paid with his head in 1747. Fraser, never a committed Jacobite but always an obedient son, had kept a low profile since the '45, during which he had led the clan

49

A private of the 2nd Royal North British Dragoons 1751.

regiment at the behest of his father. Fraser's Highlanders matched Montgomerie's in numbers, about 1,460 men, and landed with them in America in 1757. Like Montgomerie's, Fraser's had a variety of names: 2nd Highland Battalion, 63rd Foot, 78th Foot.

Besides gathering an expendable force whose savagery might reasonably be expected to match that of France's Red Indian allies, the government, by shipping Highland regiments abroad, had reduced the number of potential Jacobite rebels in the Highlands at a time when a French invasion of the south coast was expected which, if accompanied by another Jacobite rebellion in Scotland, might have been successful. It was a wonderful coincidence of interests and one which the government fully exploited for the remainder of the war.

Montgomerie's served at the assault on Fort Duquesne, now Pittsburg and lost 104 men killed and 220 wounded before going south to fight Cherokees. Fraser's accompanied Wolfe to Quebec and clinched the victory with swinging broadswords, weapons which Wolfe had seen used to great but futile purpose thirteen years before at Culloden.

In all, eleven marching regiments were raised in Scotland for the Seven Years War, only one of which was a Lowland regiment. In addition, the threat of invasion and persistent fear of Jacobitism, despite the wholesale transportation of Scotland's young men, necessitated the raising of two other regiments in the Highlands. Recruited solely for home defence and specifically only for the duration of the war, these Regiments of Defencible Men soon became known as *Fencibles*.

50

Lieutenant Valentine Chisholme, 42nd (or Royal Highland) Regiment of Foot, about 1776.

Some of these new Scots regiments served in America, some in Europe, but the 89th Regiment fought with distinction in India after it arrived there in 1761, contributing considerably to the victory at the Battle of Buxar in 1764. It was disbanded in 1765, following into oblivion the other regiments with whose services the government had dispensed after the ending of the war in Europe in 1763 and in America in 1764.

Many of the Highland regiments which had served in America were disbanded there in 1764 and were encouraged to settle; both as well-behaved tenants on lands in the Mohawk valley, and as a potential source of loyal opposition to the perceived growth of an identifiable movement for Independence.

While Highland society had been undergoing this shake-up at all levels during the Seven Years War, the conventional Scottish regiments had been distinguishing themselves in the war on the continent of Europe, in the West Indies and in the Mediterranean. The necessity of keeping virtually all the Army abroad had meant that the only force which existed for home defence was the Militia. However, fears of Jacobitism and the existence of the Fencibles, each of whose officers were carefully vetted before being commissioned, prevented the existence of the Militia in Scotland.

Government continued to resist calls by the Army for barrack-building, supposedly for fear of providing concentrations of troops in places where they could aid an insurrection but, in reality, because the billetting of soldiers in inns was cheaper in the short term. As a potential centre of rebellion, however, Scotland retained troops in barracks in

the principal towns, notably in Edinburgh and Stirling Castles and at Fort George, built after Culloden outside Inverness.

The acquisition of French territories in India and North America, the beginnings of the British Empire, indicated that the Army, although drastically diminished in size at the peace of 1763, had to be larger than that at the peace of 1748 simply in order to police the newly-acquired regions. Although America remained relatively quiet for a decade following the final crushing of France's erstwhile Indian allies led by Pontiac in 1764, Britain's involvement in India resulted in constant skirmishing in the sub-continent, the burden of much of which fell on the East India Company's forces.

The years between 1764 and 1775 were ones largely of garrison duty for the British Army: the Scots Guards were called out to fire on a mob in London in 1768, the 25th Foot garrisoned Minorca between 1768 and 1775, during which time aspects of their life there were captured in paintings. The clothing of the Army was regulated in 1768 by a Warrant which severed, once and for all, the personal connections that Colonels had with their regiments: all regiments were to be numbered, no longer were the armorial bearings of their Colonels to appear on thier Colours.

Which brings us to the American War of Independence, the added threat from the absolutist French monarchy in support of a republican movement and the resultant renewed need for a greatly-increased Army.

The conflict between King and colonists, or between the Westminster government and the Provincial Assemblies whom it pushed into rebellion by its persistently crass behaviour, produced in Scotland the same reaction as the previous war in America had. Having set a precedent in 1757 and the following five years, the government lost no time in 1775 in issuing commissions to the Scottish landowners who were anxious to receive them.

These commissions were secured by the titled and increasingly anglicised Scottish nobility at the expense of lesser landowners, some of whom spent the whole of the war pleading with Westminster to be allowed to raise regiments and redeem former indiscretions. Simon Fraser reappeared again. Restored to his estates as a reward for his service in providing men for the Seven Years War, he was a major-general by 1775 and, with the active assistance of influential friends, raised a two battalion regiment very quickly. Like its predecessor it, too, adopted the name Fraser's Highlanders but its official number was 71st in the precedence of line infantry regiments. Fraser's was one of sixteen marching regiments raised in Scotland for the war; eight of them were dignified with the title Highlanders though few, even Fraser's, were uniformly Highland in origin. In addition, three further regiments of Fencibles were raised for home defence and, in America, a regiment accurately titled the Royal Highland Emigrants was recruited from those Highlanders demobilised a decade before and settled in the Mohawk valley. Numbered 84th, it apparently sported sporrans made of racoon skin; the export of Highland dress had begun.

51

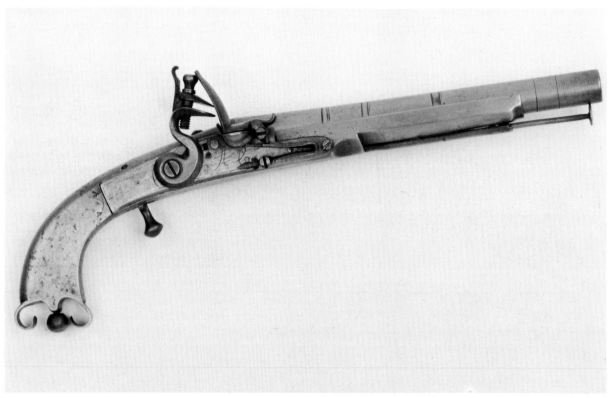

A soldier's all-steel pistol of 2nd battalion, 42nd (or Royal Highland) Regiment of Foot, about 1760.

Not all of the new Scottish regiments served in America. Some were used as garrison forces in Ireland which, at that time, was undergoing one of its periodic convulsions, some were sent to India and the beleaguered garrison on Gibraltar claimed one or two as well. In the haste to recruit, and to grab as many young men as possible, little accurate attention seems to have been paid to the niceties of explaining what military service actually entailed. There was, it must be said, a marked reluctance in Scotland to go for a soldier in 1775 and subsequent years and, in efforts to gain recruits, those charged with the task of getting as many as possible as quickly as possible almost certainly bribed and lied in order to swell the ranks. Instances are related of pressure (threats of eviction) being put on tenants by their landlords in order to get their sons into a red coat. Although such measures were chiefly confined to the Highlands, where the remnants of subservience peculiar to clan society remained, it is likely that similar measures were used further south. In any case, the misrepresentation of the realities of military life resulted in the mutinies of six regiments of Highlanders between 1778 and 1783.

The 78th, believing that they were to be sent to India instead of their actual destination (the Channel Islands), refused to go, affirming that they had enlisted for America. Promised that they would not go to India they embarked. After two years in the Channel Islands they were sent to India. The 76th were similarly confused about their destination (eventually America and surrender at York-town), and so became truculent when allowed to believe that they, too, were to be consigned to India. Drafts for the 42nd and 71st, ready to embark for America to serve, kilted, alongside fellow Highlanders, were diverted to the 83rd, a newly-raised regiment of chiefly Glaswegians, and fought with men of the South Fencibles at Leith rather than be herded aboard like sheep to serve with men in breeches whom they despised. The Argyll Fencibles took against items of their uniform and refused to soldier with them; coerced into parading to protest their grievances, the ringleaders were flogged and given to the Navy. After their comrades had tried, briefly, to hold Edinburgh Castle two further ringleaders were transported. Finally, the 77th, awaiting their expected discharge at the end of the war, mutinied upon hearing that they were under orders to sail to India, where another war was still going on. Occupying Portsmouth, their behaviour threatening to infect other eastward-bound regiments, the 77th's implacibility in the face of flagrant abuse of their terms of enlistment inspired a Parliamentary debate which overturned the Commander-in-Chief's decision. The regiment was disbanded and allowed to go home.

The mutinies of these Highland regiments were of significance to contemporary observers in an age when the soldier was generally despised and the Highlands still remote and mysterious. It was clear that the Highland soldier was not just another drunken brutal redcoat who could be flogged with impunity and sent wherever the whim

52

An example of the breech-loading rifle developed by Major Patrick Ferguson, showing the breech open, about 1776.

of government demanded. It was also clear that, if Highlanders were to be of use to the Army, they would have to be retained in regular regiments and not in ones recruited for limited service. Although the defeat in America lessened considerably the amount of territory that had to be policed by the boot and bayonet of the British soldier, sufficient troublesome Empire remained after 1783 to necessitate the retention of extra regiments.

The American experience had been more than just a proving ground for the concept of Highlanders as soldiers. The type of war fought there had transformed the British Army in many respects. Fighting against an enemy whose chief attributes were swiftness of movement, accuracy of fire and use of countryside, the British developed specialised troops to counter these. Light infantry tactics were rediscovered; having been used during the Seven Years War and having, in theory, been present in each infantry battalion since 1770, they had been neglected through lack of need. In America skirmishers and marksmen were needed as never before. Marksmen needed accurate weapons, especially against Americans armed with long-barrelled rifles, and so the *rifle* appeared, imported at first from Germany, copied in Birmingham and then issued. Five rifles per company were requested by the Highland regiments which had experienced stalkers in their ranks. All firearms issued to the Army in 1776 were muzzle-loading; they took time to load and to do so efficiently it was necessary to stand or, at least, kneel. As a result of a development by a Scot, Captain

Patrick Ferguson of the 70th Foot, of an idea by a Frenchman, a breechloading rifle was developed for the Army. Demonstrating it in 1776, Ferguson had fired 16 times in four minutes with remarkable accuracy. Although its use was limited, because of the sophistication of the weapon in the hands of none-too-careful soldiers, the Ferguson rifle and the specialist troops trained in its use achieved some success before Ferguson's death at the Battle of King's Mountain in 1780.

The American war had been, for some Scots regiments, a traumatic experience. Mustering men for a composite battalion of Foot Guards, the Scots Guards lost half their contribution from disease as well as American bullets. Disease, chiefly malaria contracted in South Carolina, incapacitated two-thirds of 71st Fraser's Highlanders in 1780. The 21st, Scots Fusiliers, was part of the garrison which, outnumbered, surrendered at Saratoga in 1777 and, having lost officers and men through privation endured in captivity and desertion to the Americans, had to be rebuilt by officers returned to Scotland in 1780.

Defeat in America had to be accepted. Defeat in India was quite another matter. When a temporary truce was patched up in 1784, the government took the opportunity to disband most of the new regiments raised to serve there but two remained which are of significance to this story. The 73rd Highlanders were raised in 1777 and advanced up the order of seniority in 1786 to 71st, later they became 1st battalion The Highland Light Infantry. The 78th Highlanders, who had gone so unwillingly to India via the Channel Islands shortly after being raised in 1778, were eventually renumbered 72nd in 1786 and became 1st battalion Seaforth Highlanders.

Warfare in the conditions in America and India had necessitated marked changes in the dress and weapons of the Scottish soldier. Most noticeable was the development of varying forms of campaigning dress. Clothing suitable, or at least not completely absurd by the standards of the time, for European warfare was patently unsuitable for American forests and dusty Indian plains. Many Highlanders, particularly officers, substituted breeches for their plaids, garments only really serviceable for the climate and terrain which produced them. The broadsword and pistols of the Highland other ranks became superseded by the musket and bayonet of the ordinary British line infantryman. The first beginnings of the feather bonnet were observable as a few Highland regiments began to adorn their headdresses with turkey feathers. In India and America, short jackets replaced coats and in India white breeches and broad-brimmed hats were worn. Like soldiers from time immemorial, the Scots in India and America adapted their clothing to suit both the climate and the fighting conditions.

While these campaigns were being fought, half a world away in each direction, Scots acted as police at home, firing as Scots Guards on Gordon Rioters in London in 1780, and as garrisons abroad in the West Indies and, notably, at Gibraltar. Gibraltar seemed constantly to be under siege during the eighteenth century; its last big one ran from 1779 until 1783, during the last year of which its garrison was augmented by the 25th Scottish Borderers. The 25th had lost its titular association with Edinburgh, the city where it was raised, in 1782 when each line regiment adopted a county affiliation which, notionally, was to be its recruiting area. For the next twenty-three years, the 25th endured the addition of: (or the Sussex) to its number: there is no reason to believe that it gained many recruits from the Brighton area.

The wars in India, which had been against Hyder Ali but continued against his son Tipu Sultan, resumed in 1787 and were to continue, virtually uninterrupted except by the occasional truce or treaty, until the overthrow of Tipu in 1799. In 1786 the 2nd battalion of the 42nd Regiment (Black Watch) had been separated from its Siamese twin and transformed into a regiment in its own right. Numbered 73rd and designated Highland it later, largely by coincidence, resumed its former role as 2nd battalion The Black Watch. The 73rd had served in India since 1782 and was not to return to Scotland until 1805, during which time it had fought in every campaign. The renewal of hostilities in India in 1787, which continued, at least ostensibly, to be aimed at protecting the position of the East India Company, necessitated the raising of further regiments. This time, seizing its opportunity to save money, government decided that, although the regiments would be raised in Britain, 2 in Scotland and 2 in England, the Company should foot the bill. Service in India continued to be so unpopular, despite the undoubted fortunes that could be made if the effects of

disease were avoided, that in order to fill the ranks of the 74th and 75th Regiments, the Company had to resort to the gaols and to out-pensioners (old soldiers) from Chelsea Hospital. The 74th Highlanders, Highlanders in dress only in many cases, survived the rigorous campaigns to become the 2nd battalion of The Highland Light Infantry. The 75th Highlanders, which had as much difficulty in justifying the description and certainly obtained many of its unwilling recruits by methods including kidnapping, recovered from the experience to become, eventually, 1st battalion The Gordon Highlanders.

The events in France in 1789 caused the hair to rise on the crowned heads of Europe. When what appeared to be a thoroughly decent and professional middle class affair was followed by the Terror and the execution of Louis XVI, even those who had thought the Revolution to be A Good Thing began to think again. The judicial decapitation of the anointed monarch accompanied fully justified fears on the part of the British government that the increasingly radical principles being expounded across the Channel might easily prove contagious in Britain. Although the degree of contagion was limited, it became common practice for the authorities to suspect any expression of anything other than the most slavish loyalty to the Establishment as outright sedition. Thus, after soldiers of the 42nd Regiment had been used to change the minds of some Ross-shire tenants who, in

Silver fittings from an officer's shoulder-belt, 71st (Highland) Regiment of Foot, about 1780.

1790, had reacted against being evicted to make room for sheep by driving off the sheep *en masse*, these dispossessed peasants were accused of republicanism. The two decades of conflict against Republican and Imperial France were to combine, without much coincidence, with fortuitous developments in the Highlands to complete the transformation of the society that had run shrieking into the musketry at Culloden.

The gradual transformation of the bleak Highland landscape from one housing far too many people scraping a poor existence from the thin soil to one whitened with the fleece of the Cheviot began in the 1790s and resulted in large-scale evictions to make room for the sheep. Those evicted were encouraged to emigrate or to settle in coastal new-towns and take up fishing. When war was declared in 1793 the process of evictions and emigrations was slowed, for fear that the supply of potential recruits would dry up. Many young men, doing as their forebears had done, went unwillingly into the Army on promises that their parents would not be evicted; all too often they were to return and find that the Cheviot munched where once their cabin had been.

The population of Highland Scotland was estimated in 1793 at 300,000 and this number was to be reduced by a tenth over the next two decades as men were drawn from it to wear The King's uniform, either as Fencible or regular

soldier. In the Lowlands too, the hunt was up for soldiers after the declaration of war and, by 1794, there were eight new regular infantry regiments (with claims of varying accuracy to be Scottish), eleven regiments of Fencible cavalry, all recruited south of the Highland line, and a similar number of Fencible infantry, all but three of which were raised in the Highlands. There were more to come.

The Fencible regiments were very much the sartorial property of their Colonels who, while nodding in the direction of the regulations governing military uniform, often embellished that of their regiments as their own fancies took them. They were aided in their concoctions by the fact that the Disarming Act of 1747 had been repealed in 1782 and Highland dress was just beginning to develop towards the peak of flamboyance that it would reach during the nineteenth century.

These regiments were the ones to whom the duty of home defence fell as the regular Army was swept abroad, to the Mediterranean, to Flanders and to the West Indies in a series of costly, and almost uniformly disastrous, adventures. Such was the eagerness to raise Fencible regiments that promises were made which could never hope to be kept under conditions of national emergency and, when many were broken, some regiments again took the road of mutiny. Thus, while the Scots Greys, Scots Guards, Royal Scots and Scottish Borderers were floundering in the mire of Flanders, incompetently led by a Royal prince, The Duke of York, some Fencible soldiers were rampaging around Edinburgh, Glasgow, Dumfries and Linlithgow threatening to shoot their officers and go home. No wonder the government was panicky. Under the circumstances, they must have been grateful for the fact that a start was being made to a programme of barrack-building, begun in 1792, which would, potentially, turn Britain into the armed camp that Ireland and, to a lesser extent, Scotland had been for some time.

During the last seven years of the eighteenth century the roll of the Scottish regiments was completed. The 78th Highlanders, raised by Lord Seaforth in 1793, became 2nd battalion The Seaforth Highlanders. The 79th Highlanders, or Cameronian Volunteers, were raised in 1793 too by Allan Cameron of Erracht; they became better known as the Cameron Highlanders. In 1794 Thomas Graham of Balgowan returned home to Perthshire after experiencing the siege of Toulon and the death of his wife, whose coffin had been desecrated by French revolutionaries. He sought and received permission to raise a regiment and did so in three months. Principally Lowland in composition, it was given the title of 90th (Perthshire Volunteers) and later became 2nd battalion The Cameronians. The 98th Highlanders, commanded by a Campbell and numbering fourteen other Campbells among their officers (four of whom were called Archibald Campbell), were raised in 1794, renumbered 91st in 1798 and eventually became 1st battalion. The Argyll and Sutherland Highlanders. Armed with a purse full of shillings, or a guinea for the more recalcitrant, the Duchess of Gordon is said to have offered a kiss as well to any man who would join the regiment she was

54

Infantry officer's sword, about 1750.

helping her son to raise. Whatever methods were used, the regiment was raised, principally from men of north-east Scotland, in four months of 1794, numbered 100th, renumbered 92nd four years later and was to become 2nd battalion The Gordon Highlanders. Finally, the 93rd Highlanders were raised, not without difficulty and a degree of coercion, in Sutherland and Caithness; they became 2nd battalion The Argyll and Sutherland Highlanders.

In 1766 William Pitt, later to become Earl of Chatham, had stood in the chamber of the House of Commons and claimed to have been the first person in government to have recognised and drawn upon the warrior potential of the 'hardy and intrepid race of men' that existed in Highland Scotland. By the end of the century, the image of the Highlander was well and truly established and, in his outlandish and eye-catching uniform, he was well on the way to adopting (in the minds of many) the role of the Scottish soldier. The growth of Empire and the movement of warfare away, in both terrain and tactics, from the billiard-table set-pieces of European war had necessitated the creation of a new type of soldier; not necessarily better, just different. This identification of suitably warlike, or martial, races was to characterise the Imperial policing policy of the British Empire throughout the nineteenth century as other equally martial races were discovered, beaten and then induced to put on British uniform. It had

been developed with the Highlander, it was perfected with the Gurkha, the Pathan, the Sikh and the Kikuyu.

Lowland Scotland was no less a valuable place for the recruiting sergeant. Just as central Scotland began to experience periods of social unrest at the end of the century, so the very real threat from revolutionary France necessitated the widespread introduction of forms of military service. Britain was put on a war footing and every man was expected to do his bit, either as a member of a Corps of Volunteers, or as a member of a Militia or Fencible regiment. The Militia had finally been introduced to Scotland in 1797 and its arrival as a concept had provoked widespread rioting. Everyone not already a Volunteer in one of the Corps that were more like posturing uniformed rifle clubs than military units had to undergo a ballot for the Militia. If selected, by drawing the short straw, the Militiaman, unlike the Fencible, could be required to serve anywhere in the United Kingdom and, in practice, probably face drafting into the regular army too. By the end of the century there were ten regiments of North British Militia, each having an aristocrat as its Colonel except the 1st (or Argyllshire) who were commanded by, yes, a Campbell.

So, in 1800, Britain faced a resurgent and revolutionary France with land forces split between the regular Army, the Fencibles (cavalry and infantry), the Yeomanry (volunteer light cavalry), the Militia and the Volunteers. Each arm was

55

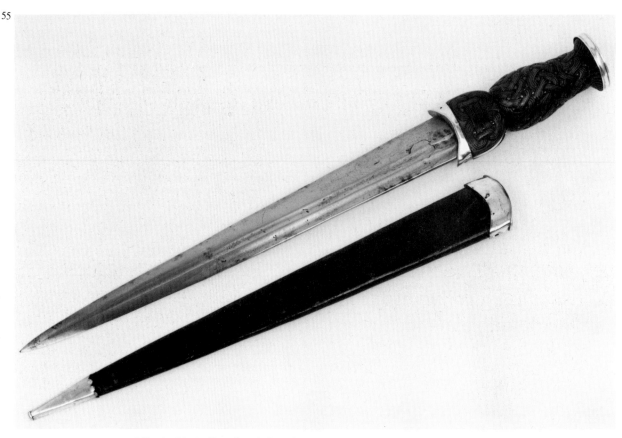

Officer's dirk, 2nd battalion, 84th Regiment of Foot, or Royal Highland Emigrants, about 1797.

anxious for recruits and each potential recruit had his preference, frequently – it often appears – to avoid as much actual soldiering as possible. The competition for recruits, the multiplication of theatres of war and the eagerness with which many seem to have avoided the temptations of a military life all combined to end the eighteenth century on a note of some trepidation for Britain. A martial race had been identified from among a fairly martial people, but would it be enough?

57

Sergeant Mather, Grenadier company, 1st Royal Edinburgh Volunteers 1796.

56

58

Officer's sword, 1st battalion, Breadalbane Fencibles, about 1793.

Officer's helmet, Perthshire Yeomanry Cavalry, about 1800.

59

Snuff mull, 2nd Battalion, 1st Brigade, Royal Perthshire Volunteers 1804.

60

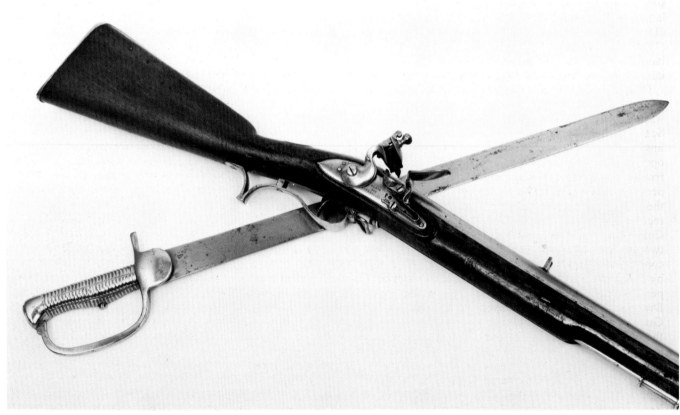

Baker rifle and bayonet, about 1803.

CHAPTER FIVE

THE WELLINGTON YEARS

1800 to 1854

If the Army of 1800 was in the grip of the greatest war for at least a century, it was at least better paid than it ever had been. Following a mutiny in the Fleet in 1797 the pay of all ranks of the Army was increased. From a sum varying between six pence (2½p) and eight pence farthing (3½p) per day, from which most was stopped to pay for his uniform and his basic food before he wore or ate either, the private soldier of the line infantry was now to receive one shilling (5p) per day. Privates of Dragoon regiments, like the Royal Scots Greys, received two shillings (10p) per day but they had to give nine pence (4p) back to pay for fodder for their horses. Privates of the Foot Guards received one shilling and a penny per day (5½p). The new rates of pay were subject to the usual deductions, or 'stoppages' in the language of the time. From his weekly pay of seven shillings (35p), the private would receive one shilling and sixpence (7½p) every week on average, out of which he could still have deducted the cost of washing and kit-cleaning materials. Dragoons were little better off.

Officers' pay rose too, particularly for subalterns whose poverty – in the case of those not having private means – was well known. The commanding officer of the Royal Scots Greys could expect to receive one pound, twelve shillings and ten pence (£1.64) pay and allowances each day. His opposite number, commanding the Scots Guards, would receive one pound, ten shillings and six pence (£1.52½) personal subsistence, to which he could add an allowance of the daily pay of one Warrant Man per company of his regiment: the tidy sum of £6.60 per day extra. The poor Colonel of a line regiment had to make do on one pound, two shillings and six pence per day (£1.12½) but was compensated for not having Warrant Men in his regiment by being able to claim a daily allowance of six pence (2½p) per company: on average about 35p per day extra. The Dragoon subaltern now received eight shillings (40p), the Guards subaltern four shillings and six pence (22½p) and the line infantry subaltern four shillings and eight pence (23p) each day. It was, by previous standards, a truly plutocratic Army.

The Army of 1800 numbered about 150,000 men. This figure did not include the Militia, the Fencibles or the Yeomanry and Volunteers. Recruits were still very hard to find and a recent Act of Parliament had empowered government to draft men from the Militia into the Regular Army; little wonder that Volunteering, which provided exemption from the Militia, remained as popular as ever.

The state of the Army in 1800 owed little to the exigencies of the war that had by then been in progress for seven years. Although cavalry regiments had been issued with new drill manuals and instructed in new sword exercises, there was no training in scouting or reconnaissance and the uniform remained as impractical as ever.

A series of defeats at the hands of the French, whose revolutionary spirit had passed from the political to the military arena, began gradually to make an impression upon the infantry. In 1800, after a few years of rather half-hearted experimenting, a Corps of Riflemen was formed, to be trained in the use of the new rifle. The rifle, a pattern developed by Ezekiel Baker and named after him, was reputedly more accurate than the smooth-bored musket still largely unchanged since the wars of Marlborough. With its brass-hilted sword bayonet it was the standard weapon of the Corps of Riflemen which trained detachments sent by other regiments. Of the fifteen regiments who sent men to the Corps seven were Scots and four Highland. These seven Scottish regiments who sent officers and men did so with considerable suspicion of the new weapon and its associated sniping and skirmishing tactics but the regiment that was eventually formed from what was actually intended as a training centre became The Rifle Brigade. The conventional infantry, other – of course – than the Highland regiments, remained the tightly-laced mannequins little changed in the course of the century. Although, just, their hair need no longer be powdered it still had to be greased and dragged back into a rigid, dirty, smelly prong at the back of the head called a *queue*. Corporal and capital punishment remained the standard choice of deterrent but neither were particularly effective. While the Royal Navy kept the French invader at bay, Britain became full of soldiers in camps and the government found foreign stations to send some of them.

Some aspects of the Army were becoming more civilized though. The cavalry acquired veterinary surgeons on the regimental strength and medical care of the Army as a whole improved with Army doctors being recognised and even inoculations encouraged. It was all very crude and the gulf

45

61

Soldier's shako, 1st (or the Royal) Regiment of Foot, about 1808.

62

Replica of an officer's helmet of the 90th Regiment of Foot (or Perthshire Volunteers) of about 1806.

of ignorance and incapacity still frighteningly wide by modern standards.

Bad as he had been as a fighting general, it is clear that The Duke of York was a conscientious and responsible Commander-in-Chief, although he later demonstrated a degree of irresponsibility by allowing the sale of commissions to become influenced by one of his mistresses. Before this scandal came to light, and he had to resign, he had interfered in, and generally improved, most aspects of the Army's life that were accessible to him. He founded the school that is now the Staff College in 1799; it continues to turn out Britain's staff officers. The Royal Military Academy Sandhurst owes part of its existence to The Duke, who founded a Royal Military College at Marlow in 1802.

The nineteenth century opened for the Scottish soldier in a cloud of glory and provided a welcome respite for the Army as a whole from the series of defeats that had characterised most of the fighting thus far.

A successful amphibious assault on entrenched French positions in Egypt by a force including the 42nd (Black Watch) and 90th (2nd Cameronians) was commanded by Sir Ralph Abercromby, a Scot who had been knighted for his services in Flanders and who had captured St. Lucia and Trinidad in 1795. The 42nd dashed ashore as part of the Reserve commanded by Colonel John Moore, a Glaswegian who was to perfect the concept of Light Infantry and die at Corunna seven years later as a lieutenant-general. Barely ashore, they were charged by French cavalry whom they

decimated with two fearsome volleys of musketry and then stormed on to assault infantry positions. The 90th, dressed as a Light Infantry regiment in their tight breeches, short jackets and leather helmets were apparently mistaken by another body of French cavalry for dismounted light dragoons. Thinking that unhorsed horse-soldiers would be easy meat, the French charged the 90th and received the same treatment as their colleagues who had taken on the 42nd. The action at Alexandria resulted in the award of three medals, none of which were given by the British government which was not accustomed to such rewards. The Highland Society of London, a body of expatriate Scots given to celebrating a glorious past amid mist-covered, heather-clad glens, had a medal struck for the 42nd. The Sultan of Egypt gave a gold medal to officers and the East India Company rewarded with a silver medal the troops commanded by Major General David Baird, the Scot who had finally defeated Tipu Sultan at Seringapatam in 1799.

The defeat in Egypt led to a temporary truce in the war and, with undue haste, the British government set about dismantling and standing down all the Volunteers and Fencibles who had been raised for the war. The Fencibles disappeared, never to return, but, when the peace treaty collapsed in 1803, the Volunteers returned as if they had never been away. As fears of invasion grew, and as Napoleon massed his barges in the Channel ports, so the number of Volunteers increased until, at its peak in 1805, the Volunteer Force was estimated to number perhaps

63

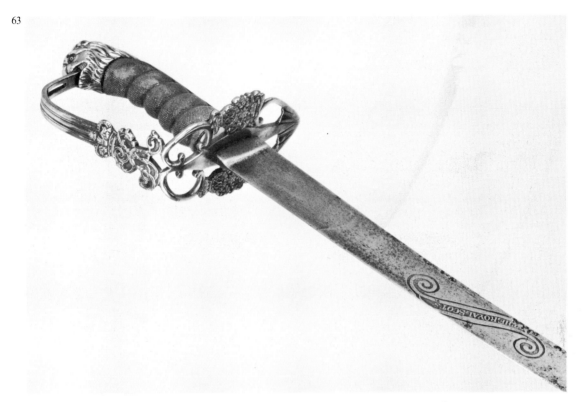

Officer's sword, Grenadier or Light Company, 1st (or the Royal) Regiment of Foot, about 1812.

400,000. The naval victory at Trafalgar, which ended ideas of an uninterrupted crossing of the Channel, finished chances of invasion and Napoleon gradually turned his armies eastward, first against Austria and then against Russia. As the barges were towed away from Boulogne so the Volunteers took life less seriously and, while they still had parades, practised with their muskets and generally strutted about to the delight of the caricaturists (and their tailors), they became even less of an effective military force than they ever had been. In 1808 the government created the Local Militia, a body distinct from the Militia – which was resurrected in 1803, which provided a method of tightening up the increasingly slack Volunteer Units. In the Local Militia, everyone able-bodied and male was ballotted and, if chosen, was liable to serve for four years after which he was still exempt from Militia service, which most people dreaded and avoided, for a further two years. The Local Militia survived until 1816 when it was disbanded after the final defeat of Napoleon.

The Yeomanry continued serenely through the period, based in rural areas and, in Scotland, always south of the mountains where the horse was part of the daily way of life for most people in the country. It was rather more aristocratic in composition than the Volunteers; its officers tended to be country gentlemen or prosperous farmers, rather than town tradesmen, and its men were their tenants. Being rural and representing the landed interest, the Yeomanry was, essentially, a mounted police force and, in the times of

internal strife that characterised the period, were frequently used to quell riots against the price of bread, or other basic grievances expressed in the usual manner by town people. Unlike the Local Militia, the Yeomanry continued in existence after 1816, although reduced in size slightly, since the threat of internal disturbances remained once Napoleonic France had been defeated.

The Militia was consolidated in 1802 and conditions of service clearly specified. The fifteen regiments of Militia in Scotland were generally organised on a county basis, small counties or counties having sparse populations being grouped together to form one regiment such as the Berwick, Haddington, Linlithgow and Peebles Militia or the Inverness, Banff, Elgin and Nairn Militia. The officers were supposed to own land in order to qualify for a commission. Colonels had to own land with a rental value of £800 Scots, lieutenant-colonels £600 Scots, majors and captains £400 Scots, lieutenants £100 Scots and ensigns £50 Scots. A stake in the country, or possessions worth defending, were felt to be an inducement, perhaps rightly, to loyalty. Everyone not exempted by service in either of the other auxiliary forces was liable to be ballotted, although one could send a substitute if chosen – assuming that one could find and bribe a substitute, and for payment of £10 one could buy exemption for five years. It was a serious business: militiamen could be transferred to the regular army or be required to serve away from home for long periods. After 1814 whole regiments could find themselves shipped overseas. In 1815 the Militia was disembodied and, although periodical ballots were enforced, notably in 1830 and 1831, it remained in abeyance until 1852 – and the next invasion scare.

The Militia took life fairly seriously; they had little choice. They were armed and dressed like real soldiers and certainly regarded themselves as such, probably to the amusement or annoyance of the genuine article. The other auxiliary forces varied but most leant heavily upon the social and sartorial side of military life. The Volunteers, often being the least military in mien and deportment of the auxiliaries, were widely lampooned for their pretensions and posturings.

In Scotland, as elsewhere in Britain, some regiments contained very rich officers, especially in Perthshire, and the amount of money that was contained in some Volunteer regiments is demonstrated by the richness of their uniforms and especially in the quality of the swords with which, it appears on every possible occasion, they presented each other. It must have, generally, been a rather agreeable experience, however ludicrous it may have appeared to outsiders, to have been a Volunteer.

In the real Army, of course, things were far less agreeable. Before the invasion of the Iberian peninsula opened what Napoleon was to call 'the Spanish ulcer' in 1808, the Army fought the French, the Spanish, the Mahrattas and the Dutch.

A campaign against the Mahrattas in India between 1803 and 1804 occupied the 74th (2nd Highland Light Infantry), 78th (2nd Seaforth Highlanders) and the 94th Regiments.

The story of the 94th is an odd one and not inappropriate to this tale. Known as The Scotch Brigade from 1793 until 1802, when it was given the precedence number 94, it was a descendant of the Scots Brigade that had fought for the Dutch since 1572. Originally of Scots mercenaries, it had been absorbed into the Dutch Army and remained there until 1783 when it was disbanded. The Scottish officers who had returned to Britain in 1783 petitioned repeatedly to bring the regiment into British service and this was allowed in 1793. It was eventually disbanded in 1818 but another 94th was raised five years later which, in 1874, was authorised to adopt the battle honours of the 94th (Scotch Brigade). This later, and last, 94th Regiment became 2nd battalion The Connaught Rangers in 1881 and was disbanded in 1922.

The 78th (2nd Seaforth Highlanders) were also in action at Maida, in Southern Italy, in 1806 when a small force commanded by Major-General John Stuart, the son of a Scot who had helped establish the colony of Georgia, embarked from British-held Sicily to the mainland and defeated a superior force of French soldiers, largely by the controlled ferocity of its aimed volleys of musketry.

Less successful was an abortive campaign in South America where a force, including the 71st (1st Highland Light Infantry), were engaged in attempting to capture Buenos Aires from the Spanish, at that time in alliance with France. Both Buenos Aires and Montevideo were eventually captured but had to be relinquished a year after being taken in 1807. Despite having the benefit of the combined talents of two of the many Scots to become eminent soldiers during the early years of the nineteenth century, Colonels Samuel Auchmuty and Robert Craufurd, the expedition was not large or well-equipped enough to retain its hold.

The South American adventure had been supplied from the garrison at the Cape of Good Hope which was commanded by Lieutenant-General Sir David Baird who had been promoted and knighted after his part in the Egyptian expedition of 1801. Baird had recaptured the Cape from the Dutch in 1806 with a force that had included his old regiment the 1st battalion 71st (1st Highland Light Infantry), 1st battalion 72nd (1st Seaforth Highlanders) and 1st battalion 93rd (2nd Argyll and Sutherland Highlanders). The 71st were packed off to South America later in the year but the remainder of the Highlanders, who at the landing had formed a Highland Brigade, remained as part of the garrison of the Cape, the 72nd for four years, the 93rd for eight. Baird received a gold-hilted sword from the City of London to commemorate the victory, which secured the route to India (and thereby the profits of the City of London).

These events, and the continuing fight against a few French and a lot of disease in the West Indies, paled into comparative insignificance beside the War that finally drained the fighting strength of France; that which began in Portugal in 1808 and spread to Spain.

Just as the later nineteenth century was to be remarkable for the large number of Anglo-Irishmen who became great soldiers, so the first decade of the century was notable for the number of eminent soldiers that Scotland produced. Most of them made it to the Peninsula but Sir Ralph Abercromby had died in Egypt in 1801. Some of these Scots we have already come across, apart from Abercromby: David Baird, Thomas Graham, Samuel Auchmuty, Robert Craufurd and John Moore, whose death at Corunna and celebrated burial have obscured for many the fact that he was both a Scot and a perfector of a system of tactics that, until he got hold of it, was little used and then to little real effect: Light Infantry. These Scots can be bracketed with others not yet mentioned, but of no less significance, like George Murray, Wellington's Quartermaster-General; Sir David Dundas, Commander-in-Chief and drill-book expert; Sir John Hope, Moore's second in command; or Sir Charles Stuart, captor of Minorca. Baird, Graham, Auchmuty, Craufurd and Moore were all to be knighted or ennobled, sometimes both, for the part that they played in the war that was known to generations during the nineteenth century, until another cataclysm took its place, as The Great War. As with that later conflict, operations outside Europe tended at the time, and later in the opinions of historians, to take second place to those conducted closer to home. The war in the Peninsula was the conflict that finally finished Napoleon. He could not conduct a war on two fronts, and after 1812 he had made the mistake of invading Russia. It says much for the fighting capacity of the French Army that it managed to sustain the onslaught from east and west for as long as it did.

Virtually all the Scottish regiments were involved in the

11

Embroidered cap of an officer of the Light Troop, 2nd (Royal North British) Dragoons, about 1760.

V

13   A grenadier of the 25th Regiment of Foot in Minorca, about 1769.

12   A soldier of a battalion company of the 25th Regiment of Foot in Minorca, about 1769.

An officer of the 42nd (or Royal Highland) Regiment of Foot, about 1790.

15

A sergeant of the 42nd (or Royal Highland) Regiment of Foot, about 1790.

14

A gold-hilted smallsword, its hilt decorated with diamonds and enamels, presented to Major General David Baird by the Field officers who served with him at the capture of the fortress of Seringapatam in India 1799, together with the gold medal awarded to him for the same action by the East India Company.

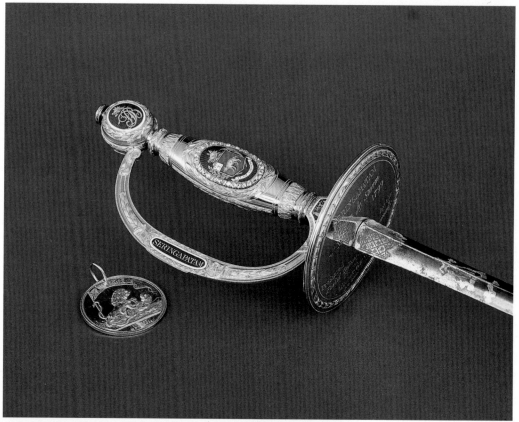

16

17

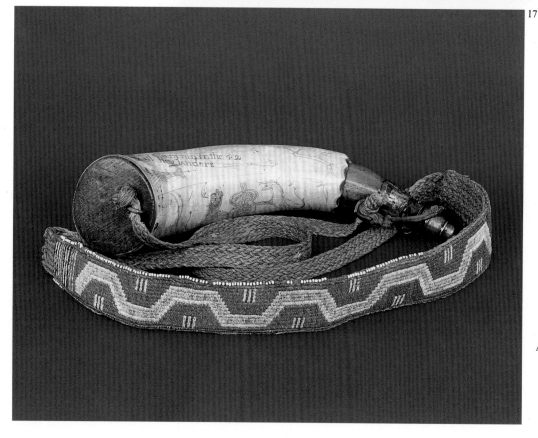

A soldier's powder-horn, carved in America in 1758 and later carried by a soldier of the 42nd (or Royal Highland) Regiment of Foot. It bears for a carrying-strap an Iroquois or Huron woman's burden strap of moose-hair embroidery and trade beads.

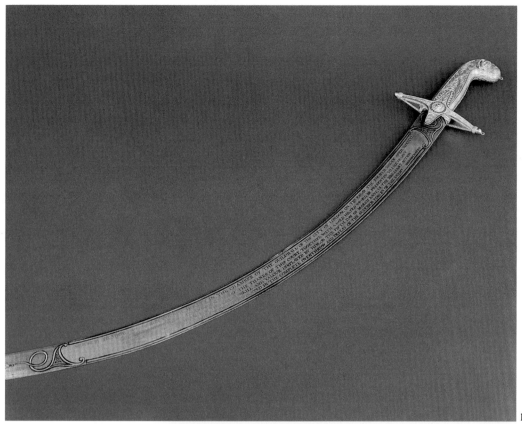

Sword presented to Lieutenant-
General Thomas Graham by the
City of London, together with the
Freedom of the City, to celebrate
his victory at the Battle of Barrossa,
1811.

18

19

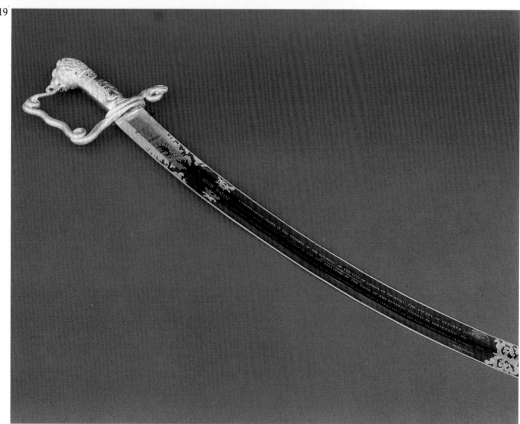

Sword presented to Lieutenant-
General Sir David Baird Bart, by
the City of London for his capture
of the Cape of Good Hope, 1806.

Piper George Clark of the 71st (Highland) Regiment of Foot continuing to play his bagpipes, and encourage his comrades, although wounded in the legs at the Battle of Vimiera, Portugal 1808.

Wounded soldiers arriving in Brussels after the Battle of Waterloo 1815.

21

22

A French caricature demonstrating the use of the kilt for collecting roast chestnuts, while punning on the effect upon the wearer's anatomy and upon female observers. Published while Highland troops were in occupation of Paris in 1816.

A French caricature indicating the fascination that the kilted Highland soldiers were reputed to have for the less discerning female inhabitants of Paris. Published while Highland troops were in occupation of Paris in 1816.

23

24

The Eagle from the staff of the French 45th Infantry regiment's standard, captured by Sergeant Charles Ewart, 2nd (or Royal North British) Regiment of Dragoons at the Battle of Waterloo, 1815.

Peninsula at some time or other. The Scots Guards, Royal Scots, Black Watch, Highland Light Infantry, Cameron Highlanders, Gordon Highlanders (2nd battalion), Argyll and Sutherland Highlanders (1st battalion) and 94th Scotch Brigade had battalions that went right through the entire war.

Some avoided the Peninsula entirely; the 1st Royal Scots Fusiliers spent most of the period in the Mediterranean, attacking Sicily in 1809 and Genoa in 1810, North America was their next campaign; the 2nd battalion became involved in the abortive raid on Bergen-op-Zoom in the Low Countries in 1813 after garrison service in Ireland for seven years. The King's Own Scottish Borderers remained in the West Indies from 1809 until 1817, aiding in the capture of Martinique and Guadeloupe. The 1st battalion The Cameronians, after participating in the fighting withdrawal to Corunna in 1809, helped attack Walcheren later the same year after which, despite a brief return to the Peninsula, it was used as a garrison force in Jersey and Gibraltar. The 2nd battalion went to the West Indies in 1805, attacked Martinique and Guadeloupe in 1809 and 1810 and then went off to Canada in 1814. The 1st Seaforths remained in Cape Town the whole time, attacking Mauritius in 1810, and the 2nd battalion was divided between the East Indies, Egypt and the Walcheren expedition. The 73rd, later 2nd Black Watch, was divided between Australia and Sweden. After home garrison duty, the 75th, 1st Gordon High-landers, took part in the occupation of Sicily in 1811, moving to Corfu in 1814. The 93rd, 2nd Argyll and Sutherland Highlanders, remained garrisoning the Cape of Good Hope.

The war necessitated vastly and rapidly increased battalions and, as an inducement to recruiting into some Highland regiments it was decided in 1809 that the 72nd (1st Seaforths), 73rd (2nd Black Watch), 74th (2nd Highland Light Infantry), 75th (1st Gordon Highlanders) and 91st (1st Argyll and Sutherland Highlanders) would all cease to wear the kilt. This item of clothing had developed from the plaid in the late eighteenth century and was, by 1809, the pleated wrap-around skirt that is familiar today, but worn rather shorter than is fashionable by both genuine and pretend Highlanders nowadays. It is clear that the supply of recruits in the Highlands had dried up and, in order to induce Englishmen, Lowlanders and others not attracted by the concept of bare knees, the government abolished Highland dress and replaced it with the standard grey trousers. This abolition remained current long after the war which originally necessitated it had finished. In addition to the loss of Highland dress by the above five regiments, the 71st (1st Highland Light Infantry) were officially transformed into the Light Infantry role in 1809 and, while retaining the title 'Highland', lost the kilt too. As a Light Infantry regiment they wore trousers or breeches and boots and a *shako*, a cylindrical hat with a peak, modified by the 71st by having a chequered band at its base, as had had the feather bonnets they relinquished at their change of status.

The fact that the 21st (Royal Scots Fusiliers) did not look especially Scottish may have saved that regiment from later calumny directed across the Atlantic at them. In 1814 the regiment crossed the Herring Pond to join the British forces busily engaged in wiping out the humiliations of 1776 and All That. After beating the Americans at Bladensburg, the 21st helped burn the government buildings in Washington, skirted strongly-held Baltimore and then marched south to waste their energies assaulting New Orleans where they lost 73 killed, 166 wounded and 238 made prisoner. A brass drum associated with the 21st's involvement in America in 1814 is still preserved in the National Museum of American History in Washington.

Devotees of the Scottish cavalryman may be wondering what the Royal Scots Greys were doing during the momentous events of the first decade of the nineteenth century. Since leaving the campaign in Flanders in 1793, where they had distinguished themselves by breaking into three enemy infantry squares, the regiment had been confined to home service, its numbers fluctuating as the possibility of foreign service advanced or retreated. One of the great moments in the regiment's history, and a watershed in the history of Europe, occurred after the return from exile in Elba of Napoleon in 1815; the battle of Waterloo.

Scottish regiments contributed 6070 officers and men to the battle, for 436 of whom it represented the last day of their lives. They may have been the lucky ones, luckier certainly than the 2093 of their comrades who were wounded in the same engagement. Some came off comparatively lightly. The 1st 91st (1st Argyll and Suther-land Highlanders) spent most of the battle on the extreme right flank with other regiments in the 6th British Brigade of the 4th Division; their casualties were five killed and eight wounded out of a regimental strength of 824. Some were savagely dealt with. The three Highland regiments at the battle all formed part of the 5th Division commanded by the Welshman Lieutenant-General Sir Thomas Picton, who wore a tall hat and carried an umbrella at his last battle; he was killed at the head of his troops. The 1st 42nd (1st Black Watch) lost 50 killed and 287 wounded out of a strength of 526; the 1st 79th (Cameron Highlanders) lost 60 killed and 417 wounded out of a strength of 703; the 1st 92nd (2nd Gordon Highlanders) lost 51 killed and 349 wounded out of 588.

Only one of the Scottish regiments reversed the usual ratio of killed to wounded. The Royal Scots Greys formed part of the 2nd (or Union) Brigade, so called because the Greys were brigaded with an English regiment, (1st or Royal Dragoons – now part of The Blues and Royals), and an Irish regiment (6th Inniskilling Dragoons – now part of the 5th Royal Inniskilling Dragoon Guards), thereby symbolising the Union of the three kingdoms which had taken place in 1801. Cavalry as a whole was Wellington's least favourite arm because of its capacity for becoming ungovernable once out of reach and this is what accounted for the Greys' casualty figures, 102 killed and 98 wounded out of a regimental strength of 391. A brigade of French infantry had been put off its stride by the musketry of the 9th Brigade, containing 3rd Royal Scots as well as the 42nd and

64

65

Brass kettle-drum said to have been left by the 21st Regiment of Foot (Royal North British Fusiliers) after the Battle of Bladensberg 1814.

A private of the 2nd (or Royal North British) Regiment of Dragoons, about 1812.

92nd, and the Union Brigade was ordered to complete the rout by falling upon the disordered footsoldiers. They did so with alacrity and cut through the infantry in a wild, thundering, slashing storm of horseflesh and steel that cost them few casualties. Then they did what Wellington's cavalry had done to him, and themselves, time and again during the Peninsular campaign; they kept going. Not stopping to regroup, or not able to stop, they thundered on until the horses were blown and they were out of reach of support. Whereupon they, in turn, were fallen upon by French cavalry, sniped at by French muskets and suffered most of their casualties in consequence.

The standard of the French 45th Infantry regiment was captured by Sergeant Ewart of the Greys during the early part of the action; he described his efforts to secure and keep his trophy in terms that still chill by their very, matter-of-factness.

'I cut him [the standard-bearer] through the head ... one of their Lancers threw his lance at me but missed ... I cut him through the chin upwards ... a foot soldier charged me with his bayonet ... I ... cut him down through the head'

The standard and the sword said to have been used by Ewart in doing all this cranial division are preserved in Edinburgh Castle; the flag is now a poor and tattered thing and the sword, the standard pattern for heavy cavalry of its

day, has all the subtlety and grace of a meat cleaver – which is generally how it was used. Because, however, it was frequently blunted either by its steel scabbard or its contact with its first couple of customrs it was not that effective a killing instrument.

The Pyrrhic achievement of the Greys at Waterloo was but one incident of a battle composed of thousands of incidents, several for each of its participants. Such is the nature of battles. As with all previous and future battles and campaigns of the British Army, it cannot and should not be assumed that the Scottish regiments involved were uniformly Scots in composition or that there were no elsewhere, serving in non-Scottish regiments. A prime example of this apparent Scottish talent for turning up all over the place was James MacDonnell of Glengarry. As a major in 1806 he had been with the 78th (2nd Seaforths) at the action at Maida in Southern Italy. At Waterloo he was a lieutenant-colonel in the Coldstream Guards, commanding the light companies of the three regiments of Foot Guards in the defence of the Chateau of Hougoumont, the courtyard gates of which he and a Scottish sergeant of the Coldstream, John Graham, closed against a great press of French soldiers eager to enter in order to set about the small garrison. The Scots Guards, aside from having their Light Company detached to defent Hougoumont, were the largest Foot Guards contingent at Waterloo, the 2nd battalion providing 1061 men 42 of whom were killed with 204

66

Sergeant Charles Ewart, 2nd (or Royal North British) Regiment of Dragoons, capturing the standard of the French 45th infantry regiment at the Battle of Waterloo.

67

Sword used by Sergeant Charles Ewart at the Battle of Waterloo.

wounded. Two of Wellington's Scots Guards aides-de-camp were also killed during the battle.

The Royal Scots were the only Scottish line regiment to have more than two battalions during the Napoleonic Wars and the 3rd battalion was engaged at both Quatre Bras on 16 June 1815, where it lost 218 men as casualties, and Waterloo, two days later, where its losses were 144.

Waterloo was more than just a watershed in the history of Europe; it created mythologies within the Army and about soldiers. In a way that was to become increasingly familiar throughout the nineteenth century, the Scottish soldier was heavily embroiled in the myth-making although, one likes (naively) to hope, not actively instrumental in it. The story about the Royal Scots ensign, killed while carrying The King's Colour and being carried, together with the Colour, away from advancing French troops by a sergeant of the regiment who was left unharmed by the French for entirely, if uncharacteristically, chivalrous reasons is but one of the stories that Waterloo produced. Only when one hears that both the Gordon Highlanders and Black Watch also claim the incident for themselves does one begin to doubt its veracity. It is also difficult to equate this apparent demonstration of French good-manners with the horror-stories circulated about quite different behaviour on the part of the enemy after the battle. But these are the stories that give regiments their all-important traditions, which are part of their strength, and so accuracy is, perhaps, not that

important. A similar case might be the incident portrayed and reproduced throughout the nineteenth century by a series of, obviously non-equestrian, artists: the supposed 'stirrup-charge' of the 92nd (2nd Gordon Highlanders) with the Greys at the beginning of the Union Brigade action. The story, which has led to an all-important link between the two regiments ever since it became current (and probably grew with the telling), goes that, when the Greys advanced through the 9th Brigade, of which the 92nd were a part, some Highlanders grasped the stirrup-leathers and were carried forward in the charge, such was their eagerness to get among the enemy. No-one with any sense would doubt the sheer hard-headed gutsiness of the average Gordon Highlander, then or now, but the fact remains that what is supposed to have happened is impossible. Even allowing that the supposed charge was probably delivered at a canter rather than a flat-out gallop, certainly at the start, the fact is that horses bunch together under such circumstances – of noise, terror and sheer impetus – so any soldier of the 92nd who was actually strong enough to hang on to a stirrup leather would either have been crushed or trampled very quickly. Given that any trained cavalry trooper would have allowed his horse's equilibrium to have been upset by the weight of a grimacing Aberdonian on one side, in order to be there in the first place the said grimacer would have had to have broken out of his line and that deed alone would have earned him a place at the flogging triangle. Such stories, however, fed the growing interest in Scottish soldiers, especially – if not solely – those in kilts, and French print-sellers, a breed renowned for their subtlety, had a field day feeding public speculation when the Highlanders formed part of the Army of Occupation in Paris after Waterloo.

Waterloo was not all myth and glory however (assuming that the business of death is ever glorious). The reality was very different. For the 71st (1st Highland Light Infantry) the breakfast that they ate, sitting on their knapsacks after a night of frequent downpours in the open, was their first meal for forty-eight hours; they had marched for a day and a half, virtually non-stop, to get to the battle in time. They were to stand or lie in the open and be shelled by French artillery a few hours after their coffee and bread and to receive constant attacks from French cavalry thereafter, losing 25 men killed and 174 wounded out of the 810 men who had marched through the night without food. The 73rd (2nd Black Watch), whose resemblance to a Scottish regiment by 1815 was almost less than notional, shared in the final rout of the columns of the Imperial Guard but not before being badly mauled by the Guard's Grenadiers when they suffered the majority of their casualties of 60 killed and 235 wounded out of 563 men.

The victory at Waterloo, after more than two decades of almost continual war, introduced nearly forty years of peace

for Britain within Europe. Although the Napoleonic Wars were not total wars in the sense that the phrase came to mean in the twentieth century, with the wholesale involvement of the civilian population, they did – eventually – necessitate a form of conscription and did, necessarily, affect the civilian population, especially those on the poverty line for whom the price of bread was all important. The ending of the Wars meant, amongst other things, that supplies of burgundy, claret and cognac could be resumed, but the price of bread continued to be an emotive issue and, when – as usual – the Army was swingeingly cut back after 1815, the threat of civil disobedience remained and so, therefore, (alone of the auxiliary forces) did the Yeomanry.

The Army's strength was reduced in 1816 to 225,000, half that of its strength two years before. By the death of George III in 1820, it had been further cut, to 100,000 men. Of those, half were in garrisons at home, in Britain and Ireland, and half abroad in India and in territories that would eventually become fully-organised colonies. The Duke of York had been reinstated as Commander-in-Chief in 1811, the British memory for scandal being as short as ever, and was to remain so until his death in 1827. Thereafter the post was to be held by Lord Hill, a colleague and protege of Wellington, and, from 1842 to 1852, by Wellington himself. The period between the battle of Waterloo and the beginning of the Crimean War in 1854 has traditionally been regarded as

Closing the gates at the Chateau of Hougoumont, Battle of Waterloo, 1815.

Captain Thomas Brown, late 79th Regiment of Foot (Cameron Highlanders),
photographed about 1850. Captain Brown is wearing his Waterloo and
Military General Service Medals; he was wounded in the left hand at the Battle
of Quatre Bras 1815.

70

Quartermaster-Sergeant Palin, 79th Regiment of Foot (Cameron Highlanders), photographed about 1850.

71

Waterloo medal 1815 awarded to Private Donald McDonald, 1st battalion 92nd Regiment of Foot.

one when the increasingly-conservative views of Wellington about innovations in the Army held back its progress. This view, although superficially valid, ignores both the progress made in improving the soldier's lot and the fact that the British Army between 1815 and 1854 was essentially an army concentrating on its growing Imperial commitment and unprepared to fight another European war. It also fails to take into account the fact that the post-Waterloo Army gradually became far more politically-influenced than it had been, as the power over it slowly moved away from the Commander-in-Chief and towards government ministers. As politics in Britain became more sharply party-oriented, a process which was accelerated and better defined after the passage of the First Reform Bill in 1832, so it became apparent that the Army had more to fear in terms of its reform from Whig governments, who distrusted and despised soldiers, than it had from Tory ones. Wellington's ten-year sojourn as Commander-in-Chief after 1842 did nothing to reduce the process and opposition to him grew, in the Army and in both the military and civilian press as well as in the radical sections of Parliament. By the time of his death in 1852, the combination of Wellington's increasingly senile inactivity and the limited horizons of politicans had seriously weakened the capacity of the Army to fight effectively in Europe. Lessons had to be learned all over again.

It is, however, too simplistic a view to describe the Army of 1854 as little different to that of 1815. Developments, although gradual and far slower than the many potential reformers would have wished, had become apparent and these were far more than merely sartorial. In fact, in matters of uniform and, to a lesser extent, of weapons and equipment, the Army *was* little different from 1815.

Every soldier, of whatever rank, who had been at the battles of Quatre Bras, Ligny or Waterloo received a medal, the first campaign medal awarded to all ranks by the British government. Gold medals and crosses had been given to officers above the rank of major since Maida in 1806 but the awarding of medals to private soldiers was a quite new departure. Encouraged by the East India Company, the awarding of campaign medals increased throughout the period until, in 1848, thirty-four years after the last battle that it commemorated had occurred, a medal was awarded to survivors of the wars against France. Between 1815 and 1848 the government had instituted a medal for Long Service and Good Conduct, in 1830, and one for Meritorious Service, in 1845. A campaign medal had been awarded for the 1st China War in 1842, at which event the 26th (1st Cameronians) provided the sole regimental Scottish presence. Finally, at the end of the period, and after another war had necessitated the recognition of gallantry by other ranks, a medal for Distinguished Conduct joined the other silver discs that gradually came to adorn soldiers' chests.

As has been said, the soldiers' uniform remained little different in concept by 1854 from that in which he had fought in 1815. He had only one uniform and everything was done in it. Its function was still to make him smart

rather than comfortable and even the predictible interference of Prince Albert in the 1840s did little to reduce his
puppet-like appearance. The visit of King George IV to
Scotland in 1822 may have had a little to do with the 71st
(1st Highland Light Infantry) and 72nd (2nd Seaforths)
being allowed into tartan trews; a sort of half measure
between their former kilted status and the blue trousers that
the trews replaced. The 74th (2nd Highland Light Infantry)
were allowed into trews in 1845. All three regiments retained
the shako instead of the feather bonnet and so achieved a
sort of Scots version of British line infantry dress. The picturesque quality of the Highland regiments is demonstrated by
the rapidity with which those of the 92nd (2nd Gordons) were
photographed at Edinburgh Castle by the Scots pioneers of the
new apparatus, Hill and Adamson, in 1845.

The weapons which Scots soldiers took with them to the
Crimea were really sophistications of those their fathers or
grandfathers had used at Waterloo. The British Army had
adopted the percussion musket in 1839, only about 25 years
after it had been developed as a sporting gun, and by the
early 1860s it was in general issue, still with a fluted socket
bayonet. It was muzzle-loading and cumbersome but a little
more accurate and reliable than the old flintlock which it
replaced. Cavalry swords were still in the position of their
function being undecided; were they to cut or thrust with?
The result was generally a combination that was bad at both
actions and was to be so until the machine-gun rendered the
horse redundant.

Throughout the first half of the century Ireland took over
the position as a recruiting ground that Scotland, and
especially Highland Scotland, had once occupied. The
Scottish regiments found it increasingly difficult to attract
recruits and statistics demonstrate how little Scots some
Scottish regiments were by the 1840s. The 26th (1st
Cameronians) and 78th (2nd Seaforths) had had to recruit
outside Scotland since 1845; only one-third of the 74th (2nd
Highland Light Infantry) were Scots. During the mid-1830s
the 42nd (1st Black Watch) got 25% of its recruits from the
Highlands, 50% from elsewhere in Scotland and the
remainder outside. Scots remained popular as recruits in
non-Scottish regiments since, unless they were Glaswegians
– who were studiously avoided except by the more desperate
regiments, they were generally well behaved and with a high
standard of literacy. In 1830 Scots formed ten per cent of the
population of Britain and Ireland and 13½% of its army;
although the population percentage remained fairly
constant, the military percentage was dropping sharply. In
1828 the 26th (1st Cameronians), about to embark for India,
recruited heavily in Ireland and accepted drafts from other
regiments, none of them Scots. A marked reluctance to
follow the old ways was noticed in the Highlands; the drain
of the land and the replacement of people by sheep had
destroyed forever the ties that bound the Highlander to his
chief. When, in 1854 the Duke of Sutherland attempted to
raise another regiment, this time for the Crimean War, from
among his tenants he was told, bluntly, that no-one on his
Scottish estates owed him anything any more, and certainly
not military service.

72

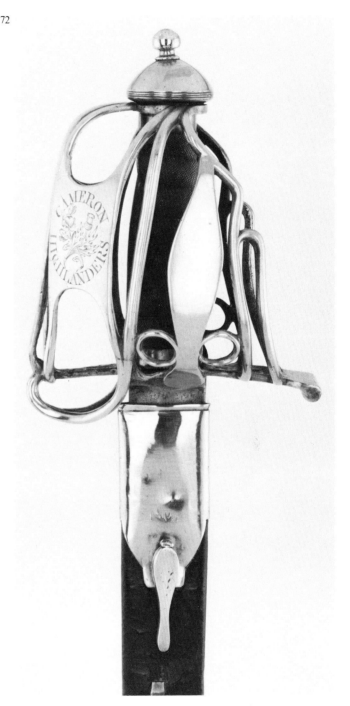

Officer's brass-hilted sword, 79th Regiment of Foot (Cameron
Highlanders), about 1820.

73

Officer's bearskin cap, 2nd (Royal North British) Regiment of Dragoons, about 1825.

74

75

Silver regimental medal awarded in the Stirlingshire
Yeomanry Cavalry, 1831.

Long Service and Good Conduct Medal, Army, awarded
to Corporal D Carroll, 42nd (or Royal Highland)
Regiment of Foot, 1837.

76

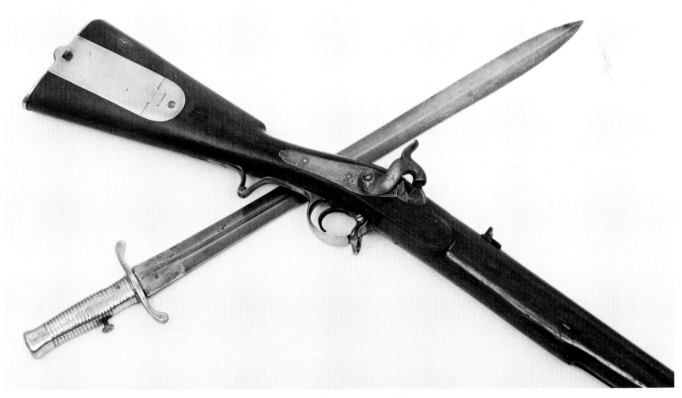

Brunswick rifle and bayonet 1843.

Other than in the service of the East India Company, Scots had little to do with the numerous campaigns in India in the 1840s. The 26th were in China, as has been mentioned, and campaigns in southern Africa, against native peoples lumped together under the title Kaffirs, occupied various Scottish regiments from 1834 to 1853. It was on the way to Africa to participate in the last of those campaigns that the troopship HMS BIRKENHEAD foundered and sank in 1852, 9 officers and 349 other ranks being lost out of 15 officers and 476 other ranks. The inadequacy of lifeboat numbers meant that those available were given over to women and children and that the soldiers, who included men of the 73rd (2nd Black Watch), 74th (2nd Highland Light Infantry) and 91st (1st Argyll and Sutherland Highlanders), had to swim for it, after allowing their dependants to use the boats unobstructed. No campaigns did not mean no deaths however; those regiments posted to India or to the West Indies almost always suffered deaths by disease. In a cholera epidemic in India in 1845, the 78th (2nd Seaforths) lost 498 men and 171 women and children to the disease, then little understood, largely incurable and almost always fatal.

The fact that women and children were available to suffer disease and death beside their husbands and fathers owed much to the liberation of the rules regarding marriage among soldiers. Although, in theory, only a limited number of wives were allowed to company soldiers overseas, in practice most went since commanding officers learnt by experience that married soldiers were more likely to be responsible and sober. Married accommodation was now provided in the new barracks being built in Britain even though, in many cases, privacy was only ensured in the barrack room by the strategic siting of a blanket.

The soldier was gradually becoming treated as a human being, and less as a marionette, more as a sensitive individual and less as a brute. It all had a long way to go however but movements to increase his sobriety, responsibility and health all reflected the fact that society, and especially an increasingly prosperous society with a growing sense of Imperial purpose, recognised that the soldier had come to stay and might well be living in barracks just down the road. The growing professionalism of the Army, while not rapidly decreasing society's attitudes to soldiers as a whole, made the institution more homogenous and therefore less subject to distinctions of nationality and regiment. While, therefore, it is still possible to talk of a Scottish soldier, it is less easy to see him as an identifiable individual of a predictable kind simply because, in the first place, the Lowland regiments looked little different in their uniforms to English, Irish or Welsh regiments and, in the second place, even soldiers in Highland regiments need not any longer be Scots. In a sense one might say that the myth of the Scottish soldier had become so entrenched that it was now difficult to tell it from reality. If this was the case, then the next sixty years would firmly weld the two together.

77

The shoulder-belt plate worn by Captain, later Colonel, E.W.C. Wright, 91st (Argyllshire) Regiment of Foot. Colonel Wright was senior surviving officer from the sinking of the troopship HMS BIRKENHEAD.

78C

Private's sword, Fife Yeomanry Cavalry, about 1835.

78A

Soldiers of all ranks of the 74th (Highland) Regiment of Foot, 1846.

78B

A piper and a drummer of the 92nd (Highland)
Regiment of Foot photographed in Edinburgh
Castle, 1846.

79

A sentry and other soldiers of the 92nd (Highland) Regiment of Foot photographed in Edinburgh Castle, 1846.

80

Soldiers of the 92nd (Highland) Regiment of Foot in undress uniform and their wives photographed in Edinburgh Castle, 1846.

CHAPTER SIX

ZENITH OF EMPIRE

1854 to 1914

Between the two British Armies that embarked for the Crimea in 1854 and France in 1914 was far more than the space of sixty years. The two bodies of men were very different and the change in the Army, in less than the span of an average human life, colossal. Both Armies were unprepared for the realities of the conflict that they were to face and both contained leaders whose tactical ideas had progressed little since their last experience of active service. There the similarities end, however, and it is debatable about how far such similarities can be pushed in any case.

Britain's role and position as a world power changed throughout the period. In 1854 she vied with France as the most powerful nation in Europe. By 1914, although pre-eminent at sea, it was very clear indeed that her Army could not, alone, match that of a united Germany.

Ready or not, the British Army plunged headlong into the Crimean War in 1854, cheered on by an exuberant public whipped to a frenzy of anti-Russian chauvinism by a ranting Press.

The war in the Crimea was remarkable for a number of reasons. It spurred on reform in the Army by revealing the neglect of the previous decade; that this neglect was revealed at all was due largely to the presence of newspaper correspondents with the Army. The incompetence and bungling that writers since have apparently regarded as unique to the Crimea were actually little worse than in previous campaigns. In those earlier campaigns though, there had been no pencil-sucking hacks present to vilify their hosts for the benefit of a growing audience of newspaper-readers at home.

The campaign was one conducted by telegraph, linking the commander in the field (eventually) with his masters in London and Paris. It produced eponyms: the Balaklava helmet, the Cardigan woollen jacket, the Raglan sleeve, a Malakoff – a type of *bombe surprise*. It produced memorable *bon mots*, usually (characteristically) in French. *On ne peut pas faire une omelette sans casser des oeufs* (Maréchal Pelissier on the appalling casualties necessary to assault the Malakoff redoubt outside Sebastopol); *c'est magnifique, mais ce n'est pas la guerre, c'est de la folie* (Général Bosquet, on witnessing the Charge of the Light Brigade). It featured battles that became streetnames or the titles of rows of middle-class villas, like Inkermann and Sebastopol, or

Christian names for children, like Alma. It created legends of heroic yet hopeless gallantry, like the Charge of the Light Brigade; it featured successes now largely forgotten, like the charge of the Heavy Brigade. It even popularised misquotations: the Thin Red Line.

It may be significant that Scots featured so conspicuously in the actions which were to make this two-year conflict so deeply-felt for a British public that was becoming increasingly aware of its Army.

Although the five light cavalry regiments which composed the Light Cavalry Brigade had no direct connection with Scotland, there is no doubt that many Scots served in their ranks simply because such was the nature of the Army at the time. A Scot lost his life at the beginning of the action that was later so movingly transformed into poetry by Tennyson. Demonstrating the facility present among Scots for turning up in the most unlikely places, Captain The Hon. Walter Charteris of the 92nd (Highland) Regiment served as aide-de-camp to his uncle, the Earl of Lucan, who commanded the Cavalry Division. Since his role would necessitate him being mounted, he had bought himself a new sword, a cavalry pattern, especially for the campaign and was astride his horse with the sword fastened to his wrist by a borrowed handkerchief at the beginning of the action. A discharge of grape-shot from one of the Russian cannon riddled his body, bent his sword and took off his head. The sword of the only Highland infantry officer to take part in the Charge of the Light Brigade is now preserved in Edinburgh Castle.

With an entirely British propensity for concentrating on defeat, the Light Cavalry action at Balaklava has tended to overshadow the successful uphill charge by the Heavy Cavalry at the same battle. In this action The Royal Scots Greys, brigaded with The Royal Dragoons and Inniskilling Dragoons, as they had been at Waterloo, in addition to the 4th and 5th Dragoon Guards, hewed and hacked their way into a mass of Russian cavalry and effectively demolished the opposition. Characteristically, the actual charge was more like a trot and, because of the bluntness of the swords carried by both sides, the actual casualties were few. The rout of the Russian cavalry was ensured by the rapid deployment of horse artillery.

Artillery were also in evidence at the other action in which Scottish participation has become legendary. At Balaklava too, the 93rd (Highland) Regiment were employed to form a fence intended to discourage another body of Russian cavalry. Only 500 strong and formed up in either four or two ranks (authorities disagree which), they presented what William Howard Russell, *The Time*'s man in the Crimea, immortalised as: 'a thin red streak tipped with a line of steel'. It is easy to see how that phrase could be misquoted. At the approach of the cavalry, moving cautiously and at no more than a canter, the 93rd, held in check by the commander of the Highland Brigade, Major-General Colin Campbell, fired three volleys. These, supported by small-shot from some cannon, discouraged the Russians from pressing home their obvious advantage over the dismounted Highlanders and added yet another phrase to the annals of British military history.

The high profiles of the Greys and 93rd Highlanders at Balaklava have tended to obscure the part played by other Scottish regiments in the Crimean War, but their deeds were little less heroic and, in many cases, far more drawn-out. The advance in line up the slope towards entrenched Russians by the 42nd (Royal Highland) Regiment at the Alma; the Scots Fusilier Guards ensigns defending their Colours at the same battle. The Guards, Royal Scots and Scots Fusiliers at Inkermann, using their bayonets in close-quarter fighting, and assisted in this butchery by the 79th Cameron Highlanders. The misery of the trenches before Sebastopol; the suffering during the Crimean winter and the gradual increase of the Army during the siege which brought the 71st Light Infantry and the 90th out to join the other Scottish infantry regiments encamped and entrenched around the city. Some of the experience gained in the Crimea would be of use in the following decades, even if much of it was instantly forgotten. For one man at least, Garnet Wolseley, who served before Sebastopol with the 90th Light Infantry, the experience of the Crimea proved traumatic. As an Anglo-Irish tradesman's son later to become (almost entirely by merit) a Viscount, a Field Marshal and one of the reformers of the late-nineteenth century Army, his service with the 90th was an auspicious start.

As has been said, public attitudes to the soldier were changing; changing very slowly. The Crimean War raised the Army's profile momentarily in a way that its involvement in a campaign closer to home than usual might be expected to guarantee. The 1850s were wedged firmly between the passage of two Parliamentary Reform Bills and the increasing self-awareness of a new type of concerned and informed middle class population in Britain meant that no longer could the Army expect to operate like an aristocratic closed shop. The influence of the Press in the Crimea, and the supposed scandals revealed – almost daily – at the breakfast tables of an increasingly-literate public, merely intensified the movements for Army reform once the Army had returned from the Crimea.

Not that all of it did return of course. Many of the soldiers still able to fight were shipped straight to India – that geographical obsession of Imperial Britain – to confront a menace that promised to present as much of a threat to Britain's position as overlord there as had the revolt of the colonists in America eighty years before. Although it would be quite incorrect to see the Indian Mutiny of 1857 as the beginning of nine decades of an Indian independence movement, the perceived ingratitude of the Indians was felt at the time to be as offensive to an increasingly aloof and paternalistic Britain as had been that of the American revolutionaries.

India in 1857 was an unhappy place. A gap between Briton and Indian that had been almost imperceptible in the 1820s and been widened into a yawning chasm by the repeated hammering in of a wedge of well-meaning but intolerant 'improvements' to Indian society by the new breed of proselytising administrators who had found their way to India in the three decades before the Mutiny. The resultant bloodbath, in which many Scots participated – both in the Armies of the Crown and those of the East India Company, was really an explosion of rage at the persistent crassness of the British administration. The Mutiny, too, produced legends – largely horrific and concerned with massacre and counter-massacre – and, unsurprisingly, one of the most enduring is that of the sound of the bagpipes of the 78th Highlanders reassuring the besieged garrison at Lucknow that help was on the way.

The Crimea, the Indian Mutiny and the Second China War of 1857–60 were all marked by the award to many soldiers of a small bronze cross. Instituted in 1856, at the suggestion of The Queen, the cross and the crimson ribbon from which soldiers wore it rapidly gained estimation and justified the capital letters and premier place among all British decorations that the Victoria Cross now holds. Its award, in the early years of its existence, was far more profligate than it has since become; not because soldiers were more brave (although they had more opportunities for demonstrating it) but simply because other decorations for gallantry were limited in number and so the VC had to cover a wide variety of types of valour. Invidious comparisons have been made since 1856 between regiments about how many VCs have been awarded to each and which can claim the most. It is no part of the function of this book to participate in the using of men's gallantry to score regimental points but it may be of interest to note that, of the 302 VCs awarded for the first three campaigns in which it was available, 44 were presented to men of Scottish regiments. Whether or not they were Scots, or whether the remaining 262 recipients of the coveted medal would claim Scots parentage or ancestry, is better left to the type of obsessive statistician for whom the Victoria Cross presents an unending fascination.

During the 1860s and '70s soldiering in Britain became steadily more civilized and concomitantly more popular. Not that recruits for the Army were more plentiful of course (they were not) but, once enlisted, the recruit would find his existence becoming gradually less disagreeable. The popularity of soldiering manifested itself in the rebirth of the Volunteer movement; part-time soldiers.

The Militia had been reactivated, to provide a force for garrison and home defence after a national, and brief, panic

81

A group of officers of the 42nd (The Royal
Highland) Regiment of Foot, photographed in the
Crimea, about 1855.

82

Soldiers of the 42nd (The Royal Highland)
Regiment of Foot, Crimea 1856.

83

A piper of the 72nd Regiment of Foot (Duke of
Albany's Own Highlanders) after return from the
Crimea, 1856.

84

Soldiers of the 72nd Regiment of Foot (Duke of
Albany's Own Highlanders) after return from the
Crimea, 1856.

about a renewed threat from across the Channel in 1852. Once that threat had subsided, the war in the Crimea loomed and necessitated the Militia's retention. Once the war was over, the continuing need for a home defence force was recognised and so the Militia remained in being. Its size, nationally, was 80,000 men and the use of the ballot was kept as a last resort, the force being recruited voluntarily. The property qualification required for a commission in the Militia was abolished in 1869 but the social status of its commissioned ranks remained largely unchanged. In 1870 Scotland possessed sixteen regiments of Militia, five of

85

The Victoria Cross awarded to Colour-Sergeant Cornelius Coghlan, 75th Regiment of Foot, 1857.

which were constituted as Artillery Militia, three dressed as Light Infantry, two calling themselves Rifle regiments and four claiming – with varying degrees of accuracy – association with the Highlands. Their Colonels included two Dukes, three Baronets and two peers' sons. It should be of no surprise to anyone who has read this far that the Lieutenant-Colonel Commandant of the Inverness, Banff, Moray and Nairn Militia (Highland Light Infantry) was the Hon. Simon Fraser. Most patrician of all was the Edinburgh, or Queen's, Regiment of Light Infantry Militia. Having the Duke of Buccleuch as its Colonel, it had a Baronet as its Lieutenant-Colonel and the Marquess of Lothian as its Major; even one of the lieutenants was a Baronet. Militia officers represented Society in uniform to an even greater extent that did Regular Army officers and it should come as no surprise that Militia soldiers were little different from their peers in the regular regiments. So similar to each other by the 1880s were the Militia and the Regular Army that the latter drew a fair proportion of its recruits, officers as well as other ranks, from the former. In any case, the Militia had worn virtually identical uniforms to the regulars since the 1830s and this practice continued until the twentieth century.

Very different indeed from both the Militia and the Regular Army were the Rifle Volunteers. One or two of the old Napoleonic-period Volunteer corps had kept together, for social purposes only, after the wholesale disbandments of 1816. Gradually these drinking-clubs diminished both in size and in interest but a few remained mildly active as rifle clubs. These existed chiefly in the south of England but there was one in Edinburgh. Whenever a national panic arose, usually because of a little light sabre-rattling from France, these clubs would offer their services to government. Both the government and the Duke of Wellington preferred, however, to rely upon the Militia which, even when it was deactivated, was potentially more governable than clutches of bloodthirsty rifle-shooters.

The last great anti-French surge of patriotism came in 1859 in response to renewed activity in Paris which seemed to indicate that France was on the move again. She was, as it happened, but not across the Channel. The failure of the feared invasion to take place did not dampen the ardour of the middle-classes who, still stirred by Deeds of British Pluck in the Crimea and in India, rushed to form themselves into patriotic groups of riflemen. These groups proliferated at alarming speed during 1859 and 1860 while the government pretended not to notice for fear of being asked to pay for them. Discouragement by default did not succeed however and the government's policy of not having a policy towards the Volunteers failed to persuade the Corps to disband. By the end of 1860 180,000 Volunteers had been enrolled throughout Britain.

The Rifle Volunteer movement has successfully defied all attempts at generalised assessment. Although, at its beginning, it was predominantly middle-class, both in inception and composition, numbers of Corps existed which were specifically recruited from both artisans (skilled workers) and the upper echelons of the professional classes. The

A trumpeter of the Royal Midlothian Yeomanry Cavalry, about 1825.

A sergeant of the Royal Midlothian Yeomanry Cavalry, about 1825.

A depiction of the 93rd (Highland) Regiment of Foot at Balaclava in the Crimea 1854: the "Thin Red Line".

Officers of Highland regiments depicted in front of Stirling Castle 1866.

Right: A sergeant and a piper of the Sutherland Rifle Volunteers 1868. The figure on the right is not a soldier but a civilian wearing formal Highland dress, possibly that of a servant of a nobleman or clan chief.

Non-commissioned officers and men of the Lothian and Berwickshire Yeomanry relaxing at Race Day on Belhaven Sands, East Lothian, 1891.

Below: Men of The Black Watch (Royal Highlanders) in a barrack room in Edinburgh Castle and about to leave for the war in Egypt 1882.

movement encouraged the polarisation of interests and was later weakeningly divided when the original cadre of middle-class support failed to cope with the increasing appeal that being a Volunteer had for the working class. Edinburgh provides an interesting example of the way in which this expression of patriotic fervour was seen as an opportunity to underline the separation of the many facets of society already existing in that clique-ridden city. Its Civil Servants, its Accountants, its Advocates, Solicitors, Bankers, Merchants and University staff all separated themselves into Rifle Volunteer Companies; further down the social scale there were companies of total abstainers and freemasons. Even in Glasgow, the journalists and accountants shunned each other when in their baggy Volunteer uniforms.

Scotland as a whole was noted as an enthusiastic centre of Volunteering and corps existed throughout the country. Alexander Henry, a noted Edinburgh gunsmith, sat up all night in order to be first on the list of a company of Volunteers and it is unlikely that he was unique. Throughout the period from 1862, after the initial enthusiastic froth had subsided and the Volunteers become properly organised into smaller, tighter units with government beginning to take a financial interest, it is notable that Scotland produced twice as many Volunteers, per head of male population, as did any other part of the United Kingdom (Volunteer Corps were not encouraged in Ireland). It is possible that this may have had a lot to do with the fact that more Volunteers came from rural areas than urban ones. Scotland was predominantly rural, especially in the north (which was

swamped with units). Even in urban Scotland more Volunteers came forward than in urban England and Wales and in London a unit was formed of expatriate Scots.

Despite the success of its recruiting in rural areas the force was a predominantly urban one. Its officers were drawn, at first, from among the growing and well-meaning middle-classes, its soldiers from the skilled working class – the artisans and mechanics. The Militia and Yeomanry remained aloof from this shopkeeper's army and that was probably one of the strongest reasons for its success. Those who were attracted to it were either unable (the officers) or unwilling (the soldiers) to enter their equivalent station in either of the other two auxiliary forces or the Regular Army. The strongest component part of the force was from young, skilled working men – a section of society which eventually came to dominate the movement and which ensured its survival once the first flush of patriotism had dispersed. The Volunteer movement exemplified the growing expression of self-improvement identifiable throughout the second half of the century. Like advances in education and the popularisation of the Arts and Sciences through the growing medium of Museums, the Rifle Volunteers owed their existence and continuation to the broadening base of British society as a whole. Patriotism was not enough; the social side of Volunteering was equally as important and the gradually-increasing links which the Volunteers had with real soldiers throughout the century brought the civilian population closer to the Regular Army than it ever had been.

It was one thing to appreciate the lot of the soldier, it was

86

A caricature lampooning the pretensions and composition of Rifle Volunteer units, about 1862.

87

Officers, 1st battalion 1st (The Royal) Regiment of Foot, Kamptee, India, 1865.

quite another to join him in the ranks however. Garnet Wolseley observed that although the Volunteers had done more than anything to make the Army popular, the low pay given to soldiers was the principal barrier to recruitment, even in Scotland.

For the greater part of the late nineteenth century only the Irish rural labourer received less pay than the ordinary British soldier. The soldier who returned from the Crimea still received one shilling and one penny (6p) per day in theory but, after deductions would be doing well if he retained three pence (1¼p). Principal deductions were for basic food, replacement of clothing and equipment, washing materials, hair-cutting and barrack damages. The latter category was a convenient catch-all that persisted well into the twentieth century. The soldiers' pay was a matter for persistent debate, along with the question of flogging, for the remainder of the century both within and outside the Army. Various measures were suggested and even attempted to resolve the problem of the low rate and the deductions. By the end of the period under review in this chapter, the soldier, still received only one shilling and three pence (6¼p) per day. His food, up to a value of five shillings (25p) per week, was – in 1914 – added to his wages and not stopped out of it.

Not only was the soldier of 1854 underpaid, he was also chronically unhealth – even at home. Descriptions of life in the barrack-rooms of the 1850s render 'squalid' a wholly

inadequate word to describe them. The death rate among the Army at home in 1857 was discovered to be higher than among any category of civilians, even coalminers. By the end of the century, due to an improvement both in the conditions and education of the soldiers, things had markedly improved and the four main killers, tuberculosis, respiratory infections, general and otherwise uncategorised 'fevers' and venereal disease, brought relatively under control. Although improvements in health throughout the nation were noticeable during the period these were quicker within the Army, largely for two reasons. One, that the Army was separate from the population and less likely to be infected by it and, two (more important), that measures identified as being beneficial to health could be imposed upon the Army and not merely recommended. The ill-health of the Army was due to two factors: indifference and ignorance. As these two factors gradually lessened so the health of the soldier improved. Indifference manifested itself in allowing barracks to be constructed with little or no thought to ventilation, heating, sewage disposal, sanitation or adequate space allowance. Ignorance was identifiable in a system which needed men to be fit yet gave them no physical training and fed them on the worst possible diet. Ignorance of the medical skills now taken for granted was a gradually-diminishing *sine qua non* throughout the period. Gradually the barracks improved: piped water arrived, latrines replaced the communal wooden urine tub and the value of

88

Officers of 72nd Regiment of Foot (Duke of Albany's Own Highlanders) within the Half-Moon Battery of Edinburgh Castle, 1866.

fresh air became appreciated. Hospitals were built, libraries and reading rooms began to sprout in garrisons and games, sports and calisthenics all became part of the soldier's life.

His service in the Army was shorter than ever by the second half of the century. Until 1847 the soldier enlisted for life, or until he was so worn out that he could be returned to the streets from whence he came. The Crimean infantryman enlisted for twenty-one years, the cavalryman for twenty-four. Each could contract for an initial period of ten and twelve years with the option of re-engagement, an option that would guarantee a pension if he survived. In 1870 the initial twelve years was made common to both cavalry and infantry but divided into six years in the Army and six years in the Reserve (liable to call-up in time of emergency). Re-engagement up to a limit of twenty-one years remained an option. In 1881 the division between the twelve years was changed from six-and-six to seven-and-five. This proportion remained the same until 1914. Standards were dropping however, as the need for more and more soldiers to police the Empire grew and, although medical examinations of potential recruits became more exacting, those recruits became shorter (as the minimum height was dropped) and more likely to be from the towns rather than the countryside.

Scotland was no longer the reservoir of manpower that it had once been and even Ireland had stopped swamping the Army with her young men as first the Famines of the 1840s and then the resulting trans-Atlantic emigrations denuded that island of her cannon-fodder. In the 21st (Royal Scots Fusiliers) in 1851 358 out of 696 soldiers were Irish, as were 34 of the 89 non-commissioned officers. Thirty years later the Irish contingent was only 20%. At the end of the century a survey of eight Scottish regiments stationed in Scotland (five of which were Highland) revealed that the Irish proportion of their complements had dropped to 4%. The 93rd (2nd Argyll and Sutherland Highlanders), regarded by many as the last bastion of the old Highland style of regiment, had 86% of its soldiers from Scotland in 1871 and 82% of its non-commissioned officers were Scots. Even in the 93rd, though, this proportion was remarkable and certainly reduced gradually as the century progressed. Figures do not indicate what proportion of the Scots were Highlanders.

The 93rd were notable too, even among Highland regiments, for their good behaviour and it seems that the whistle of the cat-of-nine-tails was a rare occurrence in that regiment. It became rarer still after the Crimea, by which time the number of lashes that could be awarded for any one crime was reduced to fifty. It may be hard to comprehend now how such a savage punishment could be regarded as an improvement but, fifty years earlier, sentences of several hundred lashes were not uncommon, often delivered, in several helpings once the recipient's back had begun to heal. The nine 'tails', or thongs, of the whip each had three knots strategically situated along the length of rawhide or

89

Carte-de-visite photographs of officers of 92nd Regiment of Foot (Gordon Highlanders),
about 1865.

whipcord. Particularly sadistic individuals charged with the task of delivering the punishment would often soak the cat in water so that the tails' cutting capacity was increased, and would perfect the art of not merely striking the soldier's back but rather drawing the cat across it as if wielding a sabre. Soldiers not infrequently died after being flogged. While some may, even today, favour this type of punishment, it should be remembered that not only could fifty lashes be inflicted largely at the whim of a regiment's Commanding Officer but also for the most trivial of offences such as insuborinate language or drunkenness. Through the 1850s, '60s and '70s, flogging was regularly debated inside and outside the Army, most frequently in Parliament on an annual basis. A questionnaire circulated to a dozen or so senior officers in 1879 asked for their reactions to the suggestion that flogging should be abolished. With one exception, all were in favour of its

retention. Even Wolseley, otherwise such a reformer, could think of no other way to discipline what he called the 'ruffians and criminals' who formed the Army's backbone. The exception was Frederick Roberts, an Anglo-Irishman who had won a Victoria Cross with the Bengal Artillery during the Mutiny and who was beyond compare as the greatest and most humane soldier of his age. He became an Earl, a Field Marshal, recipient of numerable Orders of Knighthood and the last Commander-in-Chief of the Army. Reduced to twenty-five lashes maximum in 1879, flogging was finally abolished in 1881. Gradually systems of fines for small offences and imprisonment for more serious ones came to replace the savagery that brutalised the offender and sickened those ordered to watch. Corporal punishment was retained, supposedly as a last resort, on active service however until well into the next century since it was recognised not only that an Army at the sharp end of a conflict

90

Silver statuette depicting an officer of the Royal Midlothian Yeomanry Cavalry of 1872. On the disbandment of the regiment in that year, each of the nineteen officers received one of the statuettes.

had to be tightly gripped but also that the rudiments of discipline – especially in matters affected by alcohol – tended to disperse on such occasions.

This breakdown of the tenuous thread that welded the Army together was noticeable in two campaigns at the end of the 1870s, both characterised by initial defeat and both fought at the extremity of Empire: the Second Afghan War of 1878–80 and the Zulu War of 1879.

During the latter conflict the number of incidences of flogging in the field was 500, a rise in savagery that may have owed much to the panic engendered by the slaughter of an infantry battalion by Zulus at Isandhlwana in January 1879. Whatever the reason, its apparently indiscriminate use finally destroyed the practice, at least for the peacetime Army.

The Army on campaign was a very different beast to that kept chained up at home. It received a rum ration, which necessitated vast liquid stores being transported with the soldiers; it was away from such restraining influences as might normally be exerted by its wives and its corporate adrenalin was flowing. The chaplain attached to the 72nd Highlanders for the campaign in Afghanistan was a Baptist missionary, John Gregson, who spent much of the rest of his time being Secretary (and founder) of the Soldiers' Total Abstinence Association. The Association was based in India and deliberately aimed at weakening the hold that the Demon Drink had upon British soldiers stationed in the sub-continent. It had grown steadily from its foundation in 1861 but suffered a severe set-back in Afghanistan in 1878 when, confronted with the realities of a bullet from a *jezail* or a disembowelling thrust from a *choora*, active membership of many regimental branches fell away sharply. Gregson was able in later years to wax censoriously lyrical about the spectacle of the 92nd (Gordon Highlanders)

91

1st (City of Edinburgh Rifle Volunteer Brigade) Edinburgh (City) Rifle Volunteers in camp at Ayr, 1865.

92

Captain Edward Straton, 22nd (Cheshire) Regiment of Foot and
signallers of the 72nd Regiment of Foot (Duke of Albany's Own
Highlanders), Afghanistan, 1878.

93

Officers of the 92nd Regiment of Foot (Gordon Highlanders), Afghanistan, 1878.

94

Camp of the 78th (Highlanders) Regiment of Foot (Ross-shire Buffs), Karachi 1880.

celebrating Hogmanay in 1879 with a bacchanalian frenzy that clearly appalled his English Non-conformity. Both sides of the equation were obviously reverting to type. The temperance movements in the Army were at their most effective in India, where the dual temptations of cheap alcohol and periods of idleness enforced by the climate combined to confront the Army with a perceptible drink problem. Although it is tempting to speculate otherwise, there is no evidence to suggest that the Scottish regiments were more at risk than others. If anything, the reverse seems to have been the case. Certainly, the 71st (1st Highland Light Infantry) had a regimental branch of the Total Abstinence Association during the 1870s which was held up by Gregson as a shining example of its type, both in numbers and in degree of vociferous commitment to the cause. After visiting Cairo in 1883, at Wolseley's request, to extend the mission of Army Temperance, Gregson was presented with an illuminated address by the regimental branch of the 42nd (1st Black Watch) which enthused about the extent to which he had helped lead the regiment away from liquid temptation.

The problem of alcohol abuse was not, of course, restricted to common soldiers. It was almost expected that they would become drunk and riotous on every possible occasion; hence the vocal support for the retention of flogging. In the commissioned ranks, alcohol fulfilled a similar social purpose but its consumers were expected to be discreetly circumspect when inebriated and not begin damaging each other. Boyish horseplay and a little furniture-smashing were acceptable in a society where such behaviour was little more than an extension of school. The gradual increase, after 1871, of a slightly more serious and dedicated breed of officer lessened the instances of officers being cashiered for habitual intoxication. The purchase of commissions was abolished in 1871, at an estimated cost to the Exchequer of £8 million in compensation to officers who had bought their commissions before the axe fell.

The abolition of purchase was but one of many reforms that gradually permeated the Army during the 1860s and '70s. These were all aimed, at bottom, at producing a small and efficient Army, properly armed and trained, fit, well-fed and healthy. This aim was far more than just a result of the growing interference by Parliament and Whitehall in military matters. It was a reflection, prompted by events in Europe, of the Crimean Army's inability to fight a war there against the one nation increasingly likely to be Britain's antagonist: Prussia.

In the face of transparent bluster from Palmerston, the Prime Minister, Prussia had brushed aside the Danish armies in a brief campaign aimed at resolving a dispute over the ownership of the boundary territories of Schleswig and Holstein in 1864. How much Britain's opinion mattered and, more significantly, what little Britain could do to stop a nation bent on self-determination in Europe was rapidly revealed. So was the superiority of the Prussian Army over that of Britain, still basking in a post-Waterloo twilight little obscured by the revelations of the Crimea, and comfortable in the belief that a Sunday afternoon force of baggy-

trousered tradesmen rendered her shores inviolate. If the demolition of the Danish Army in 1864 took the British government aback, then the annihilation of the Austrian Army at Sadowa in 1866 shook it rigid. In 1870 Prussia goaded France into crossing the Rhine, never a difficult task, and promptly savaged the armies of Napoleon's nephew, Napoleon III, in a campaign that supplanted the supposed continental mastery of the French Army by the real pre-eminence of the Army of the now united, and Imperial, Germany.

These three campaigns, and the bitterly destructive and divisive War between the States in America in the mid-1860s, were all observed keenly from Britain. As with all warfare they inspired, principally, huge advances in weapon technology and, less apparently, developments in strategy and tactics. They were campaigns in which breech-loading rifles were used (Prussia had had them since 1849, five years before the Crimea). In America and during the Franco-Prussian War some use was made of rudimentary but effective machine-guns: the Gatling and the *Mitrailleuse*. The early breech-loaders were clumsy single-shot affairs but afforded a far higher rate of fire than was available to the soldier armed with the muzzle-loader. The machine-gun swiftly disposed of the idea of frontal assault. When used properly, it treated men with the murderous disdain of a scythe.

Experiments with breech-loaders had been pursued in Britain during the 1850s and '60s but the Army did not receive its first breech-loading rifle until 1866. Even then it was a conversion of a pattern introduced in 1853. In 1871 its first proper breech-loader was issued to the Army, the single-shot, hammerless Martini-Henry rifle; the combination of a Austrian breech (Martini) and a Scottish barrel (Henry). Both the Snider-Enfield of 1866 and the Martini-Henry of 1871 were issued with a fluted steel socket bayonet of a type not essentially dissimilar to those first issued to the Army a century and a half before. During the 1870s Britain bought the Gatling hand-cranked machine-gun from America and used it to considerable effect in Zululand in 1879 when, on the occasions that it wasn't jammed with dust or sand, it proved an effective way of forgetting the humiliation of Isandhlwana.

Conditions in the Crimea had reduced the Army's appearance to that of a collection of tramps who had seen better days by mid-way through the campaign. It rapidly became clear (to those few who had not always known) that the clothes that looked pretty on the parade ground were of little use for fighting in. The Highland regiments went to war in the kilt, short jacket and feather bonnet: a tall, bouncy confection of ostrich feathers that was itchy in the heat and adept at collecting water (guaranteed to run down the wearer's neck) in the rain. Cavalry wore tight jackets and sported a variety of headgear; the Greys wearing a tall bearskin cap. Ordinary infantry were buttoned into tight coats, buckled into constricting belts, choked by high leather stocks and made to wear a tall shako known colloquially after the Queen's Consort and used by at least one Scottish soldier in the Crimea for collecting dried camel

95

Lieutenant-Colonel Francis Brownlow, Commanding
Officer, 72nd Regiment of Foot (Duke of Albany's Own
Highlanders), 1878.

96

Alexander Henry, the noted Edinburgh gunsmith, in the
uniform of 1st (The Queen's City of Edinburgh Rifle
Volunteer Brigade) Edinburgh Rifle Volunteers, 1880.

97

The Scots Guards, in drill order, returning from exercise preceded by their band, Hyde Park, 1880.

98

Sentry, Seaforth Highlanders (Ross-Shire Buffs, The Duke of Albany's), about 1884.

dung for a fire. It was certainly a better bucket than a hat. Things improved slightly after the war as uniforms became looser and the stock was discarded. Highlanders adopted the doublet while the rest of the Army went into the tunic but there was still really only one uniform in which the soldier did everything. More use of khaki or grey clothing was made in India, at least for the top half of the soldier, and by the 1880s issues of light-weight khaki clothing were common for troops east of Suez.

Reforms of the Army were, in view of the institution's capacity to absorb change, necessarily slow, surrounded by difficulty and prevarication, frequently obstructed, generally imposed from outside and usually unpopular within. Pre-eminent among the Army's reformers in the decades after the Crimean War was Edward Cardwell, Secretary of State for War in Gladstone's Liberal government of 1868. The majority of the reforms of the Army's organisation dealt with thus far in this chapter can be credited to his influence, although much was already under way by the time that he

Below: Cooks, 1st battalion the Cameronians (Scottish Rifles), Aldershot 1883.

99

assumed office. One of the most important developments in the history of the Army, and one which is of profound significance to this story, is usually associated with Cardwell's name but was actually carried through in 1881 by Hugh Childers, Secretary of State for War between 1880 and 1882.

These reforms transformed the line infantry regiments and amalgamated three-quarters of them to reduce their numbers from 109 marching regiments to just 69. The idea was that each of the new regiments would have one battalion abroad and another at home, training and recruiting, and that the two would periodically change places. The first 25 line infantry regiments already had two battalions and so were left untouched, for the time being. The remainder, excluding The King's Royal Rifle Corps and The Rifle Brigade, were each doubled up to form 41 new regiments. The only exception among the line infantry was the single-battalion 79th (Cameron Highlanders), which eventually raised a second battalion in 1897 to conform with the others. Once the two, frequently quite dissimilar, battalions were linked, the numbering system by which line regiments had been known for 130 years was dropped and

new regimental titles blossomed. These now, at least in Scotland, resound like a roll of sacrifice as if they were centuries old instead of a mere hundred years or so.

The 26th (Cameronians) amalgamated with the 90th (Perthshire Volunteers) to form The Cameronians (Scottish Rifles). The 42nd (Royal Highland) joined with the 73rd to form The Royal Highland Regiment (Black Watch). The 71st and 74th formed The Highland Light Infantry and the 72nd and 78th The Seaforth Highlanders (Ross-shire Buffs, The Duke of Albany's). The 75th (Stirlingshire) were swallowed whole by the 92nd (Gordon Highlanders) to form The Gordon Highlanders and, after nearly being called the Sutherland and Argyllshire Highlanders, the 91st and 93rd created The Argyll and Sutherland Highlanders.

Added to the newly-created regiments, and the older (and largely untouched) Lowland regiments, were Militia battalions formed from the Militia, which was brought much closer to the Regular Army by being given a 'parent' regiment. In addition to the Militia battalions, the Rifle Volunteers were transformed into Volunteer Battalions of 'parent' Regular regiments and, although retaining

Battalion shooting team, 1st Volunteer Battalion (Inverness Highland) The Queen's Own Cameron Highlanders, Inverness 1887.

100

vestiges of their old identities, gradually merged with the Regulars.

Scotland in 1881 was a very different place from the divided and troubled nation of a century and a half before. The fading threat of Jacobitism throughout the eighteenth century, the repeal of the Disarming Acts, the visit of King George IV in 1822 and the novels of Sir Walter Scott had all made Scotland as a whole reputable and the Highlands themselves mysterious. The phenomenal sales of Scott's novels during the nineteenth century, and the respectability conferred upon Highland Scotland by the purchase and re-building of Balmoral by The Queen in the 1850s, had combined with much typically Scottish entrepreneurship in the field of identity-invention to add Romance to the mystery. Tartan became big business and, as land-use and ownership in the Highlands changed from the old ways to the new, so Scotland, from being a tiresome frontier province, became fashionable. Representing the new fashion was the Highland soldier. By 1881, in full dress, the Highland officer demonstrated a capacity for inducing feelings of inadequacy in the most gaudy of Christmas trees (another Victorian import). With their tartan kilts and feather bonnets, with pipers and broadswords, the Highland regiments were the object of much bemused, and often bitter, envy from men of non-Highland regiments. It was felt, occasionally justifiably, that the Highlanders' part in any action tended to be disproportionately reported because their outlandish appearance and awful noise made them more noticeable.

Well placed to take advantage of the new fashion for things Scottish were the Lowland regiments who decided to get a piece of the action and used the opportunity of new uniforms (necessitated by the replacement of numbers by names) to come out as noticeably Scottish. Hitherto largely unrecognisable as Scottish, although most had had pipers since at least the 1850s, the Lowland regiments appeared with tartan trews, Highland doublets and a variety of head-dress indicating varying degrees of Lowland Scottishness. The Cameronians retained their Rifles pattern swords and drab appearance but the other Lowland regiments adopted basket-hilted claymores, broad white shoulder belts and other formerly Highland impedimenta. They lacked only the kilt and feather bonnet to resemble the sort of figure whose ancestors their ancestors had despised, feared and slaughtered but who, by 1881, had come to personify Scotland.

Between the end of the Second China War in 1860 (during which campaign The Royal Scots were the only Scottish regiment present) and the beginning of the Second Boer War in 1899, Scots fought abroad in numerous skirmishes and campaigns each, to a varying extent, concerned with either extending the frontiers of Empire or maintaining its credibility. A campaign in Canada against Fenian-inspired terrorists occupied the 25th (King's Own Scottish Borderers) in 1866; a punitive expedition against the King of Abyssinia took up a little of the time of the 26th (Cameronians) during 1867 and 1868. The 42nd (Black Watch) and some of the 79th (Camerons) participated in the Ashanti War of 1873–74. The part played by the 42nd (clad in grey for the occasion) in the assault on the Ashanti capital, Kumasi, was recorded in bloodthirsty detail by an American journalist later to be famed for his presumption: Henry M. Stanley. Bloody noses in Zululand and Afghanistan followed at the end of the 1870s; wounds which were rapidly repaired by the exertion of weight of numbers. Humiliation at the hands of the Boers in the First Boer War of 1881 involved the 92nd (Gordons) who were badly mauled at the indefensible trap which had appeared such a strongpoint and was re-membered as Majuba Hill. Imperial campaigns in Egypt and the Sudan in the 1880s and '90s drew upon many Scottish regiments, most of them Highland.

A Highland Brigade, comprising the Black Watch, Highland Light Infantry and Cameron and Gordon High-landers, was formed for the Egyptian campaign of 1882; it showed something of the spirit of its supposed ancestry when, though devoid of axes and broadswords, it took Tel-el-Kebir with the bayonet. The Black Watch remained to take part in the attempted rescue of General Gordon at Khartoum and the Camerons and Seaforths were kept busy at the battles of The Atbara and Omdurman in 1898. The Royal Scots Fusiliers were involved in Burma in 1885–87, as were The 1st King's Own Scottish Borderers a couple of years later. The 2nd King's Own Scottish Borderers joined the 1st Gordons during the North-West Frontier campaign of 1897–98 where, at Dargai, the Highlanders were given moral support by the bagpipes played by Piper George Findlater who was awarded the Victoria Cross for con-tinuing to play while immobilised with ankles shattered by bullets.

Virtually every Scottish regiment was represented by one battalion or another during the Second Boer War of 1899–1902; the 1st Scots Guards formed part of the Guards Brigade and the Greys part of 1st Cavalry Division. The Highland Brigade, composed of 2nd Black Watch, Highland Light Infantry, 2nd Seaforth Highlanders, 1st Gordon Highlanders and 2nd Argyll and Sutherland High-landers suffered appalling casualties at Magersfontein at the end of 1899 and all Scotland was plunged into mourning. Advancing, close together, towards entrenched Boer posi-tions across flat ground laced with barbed wire and with no cover, they were first fired upon accurately and heavily and then forced to lie in the rising sun and be picked off one at a time. Total casualties were barely less than a thousand men; the Black Watch lost over 300, it was another Ticonderoga for them.

The reverses of the first four weeks of the war appalled the British public who, forgetting Majuba Hill, had expected the Boers to be as much of a pushover as had been the majority of other enemies against whom their Army had fought in recent years. The revelation that the Regulars had a fight on their hands, and an unconventional one at that, inspired a surge of patriotism and Volunteers rushed to offer their services. Fortunately, few were allowed to endanger the lives of the regulars by their presence in the ranks of the infantry since their training, although supposedly allied to that of the Regulars, had not fitted them for active service.

101

Soldiers of 1st battalion The Royal Scots (Lothian Regiment), breaking for a rest and food during exercises in Natal, about 1890.

102

Staff-Sergeant (Musketry) Ferguson and his son with Staff Sergeant Campbell, Prince Louise's (Argyll and Sutherland Highlanders), Kinross Camp, 1890.

For the Yeomanry however, the opportunity was tailor-made. Largely unused as a police force since the Crimea, their function had been generally decorative for several decades. The need for competent horsemen in South Africa resulted in the raising of Imperial Yeomanry battalions which were volunteer units numbered rather than named – in general – but based upon the county-oriented Yeomanry Cavalry regiments. The Ayrshire Yeomanry Cavalry, for instance, formed the 17th Company of the 6th battalion and, in two contingents, a total of 1,600 men fought in South Africa. In addition to the Scottish Imperial Yeomanry Companies, two entire regiments of Yeomanry were raised of Volunteers for the war: the Lovat Scouts raised by Lord Lovat (emulating his predecessors) and the Scottish Horse raised by the Marquess of Tullibardine, heir to the Duke of Atholl.

The acceptance of the services of these auxiliary units was itself an admission that the Regular Army could not cope with unconventional warfare against well-equipped and armed troops. Serious doubts were raised too about its capacity to fight a conventional (European) war. Just as the Crimean War had led to decades of introspection and gradual comprehension, so the war narrowly won (or drawn) in South Africa led, eventually, to the reforms that would produce the Army of 1914.

The Army in South Africa was a khaki-clad army. Although the Highland Brigade had died in the dust of Magersfontein in their kilts, their jackets were khaki and their heads protected from the sun by khaki sun-helmets. Since 1881 they had been armed with repeating rifles and in 1892 the words 'Lee-Enfield' first applied to the weapon of the British infantryman. In 1902 khaki service dress was adopted by the entire Army, full dress being retained until 1914 by the soldiers for special occasions. The distinction between the cavalryman's carbine and the infantryman's rifle was done away with by the issue of a shortened version of the Lee-Enfield rifle used in South Africa. Firing a small calibre bullet, it had a magazine containing ten rounds and was fitted with a sword-bayonet. It remained the standard weapon from about 1902 until the early years of the Second World War for both infantry and cavalry. Training was improved and a vast area of land north of Salisbury in Wiltshire brought into use as a training area where preparations for what seemed to be the inevitable European War were made. The government of the Army was radically overhauled, an Army Council created to oversee Parliamentary control and the administration of the War Office re-shaped. All this in the space of two years, from 1902 to 1904.

When the Liberal government of 1906 took office, much of the necessary background work for wholesale reform of the Army had been done. A Scottish Secretary of State for War, Edward Haldane, polished off what was left. Assisted in his task by a Scottish cavalryman with South African experience, Douglas Haig, Haldane began work on the system proposed by one of his predecessors Arnold-Forster, for a Home Service Army that would support the Regulars in time of war. He created the Territorial Force in 1908 out of the Volunteer Battalions and the Special Reserve out of the Militia Battalions. The object of the exercise was to construct a system whereby an Expeditionary Force could be thrown across the Channel in two weeks and be fed from a Reserve force at home. Haldane completed the task that had been begun by his predecessors. He was the architect of the Army that took ship for Flanders in August 1914, a month after the death knell of civilization had been sounded by the revolver shots at Sarajevo.

Association Football team of The Royal Scots (Lothian Regiment), Champions of India 1894-95.

103

104

Soldier's tropical helmet, Gordon Highlanders, about 1897.

105

Bagpipes played by Lance-Corporal Piper Patrick Milne, 1st battalion Gordon Highlanders, at the Battle of Dargai on the North West Frontier of India, 1897. Milne received a Distinguished Conduct Medal personally from The Queen for his bravery at the battle.

106

Sergeant, The Royal Scots Fusiliers, about 1898.

107

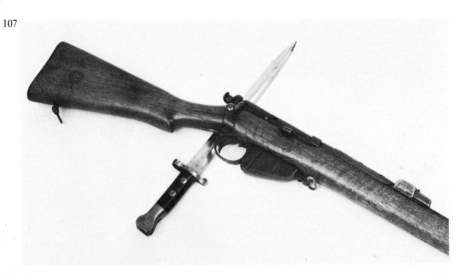

Lee-Enfield Mark I magazine-loading rifle and bayonet, 1898.

108

Officers of the 2nd Dragoons (Royal Scots Greys) on active service in South Africa 1901.

109

110

Lieutenant-Colonel Claud Laurie of Maxwelltown DSO, Commanding Officer, 3rd Militia Battalion, The King's Own Scottish Borderers, about 1904.

The Regimental Sergeant-Major, Princess Louise's (Argyll and Sutherland Highlanders) 1906.

111

Soldiers of the 1st battalion The Highland Light Infantry in khaki jackets and tartan shorts,
India, 1906.

112

Pioneers of 2nd battalion, The Highland Light Infantry, about 1907.

113

Webley Mark VI. 45 calibre revolver, about 1914.

114

Short Magazine Lee-Enfield rifle and bayonet 1915.

CHAPTER SEVEN

THE FLOWERS OF THE FOREST

1914 to 1918

In 1913 Scotland was represented in 7.6% of the Regular Army, both by the Scottish regiments themselves and by Scots serving elsewhere in the Army. Ireland, by contrast, provided just over 9% of the Army. During the four years of war 557,618 Scots enlisted into the Army, a figure that represented 41.4% of males between the ages of 15 and 49 in Scotland and 23.7% of *all* males in Scotland. By contrast, although by far more men enlisted into the Army from England and Wales, their proportions per head of population were only fractionally more than that of Scotland. In fact, during the period up to January 1916, when enlistment was voluntary and conscription still not introduced, Scotland's recruits exceeded, per head of male population between 15 and 49, those of both England and Wales together. Only when conscription was introduced, in 1916, did Scotland's contribution fall below that of England and Wales. It always far outstripped that of Ireland but then Ireland had troubles of its own.

These men eventually comprised six infantry divisions. Two were formed from the New Armies raised after the British Expeditionary Force had proved unequal to the task of driving back the German armies. The 9th and 15th Divisions both came into being as a direct result of the appeal by Lord Kitchener and the realisation of the recruits that Their Country Needed Them. The 51st (Highland) and 52nd (Lowland) Divisions were divisions formed from the Territorial Force before the outbreak of war and the 64th (2nd Highland) and 65th (2nd Lowland) Divisions were authorised to be raised from the Territorials in September 1914. The 1st battalion Scots Guards went to France with 1st Black Watch in 1914 as part of 1st (Guards) Brigade of the 1st Division; the 2nd battalion joined the 2nd Gordon Highlanders as part of 20th Infantry Brigade in the 7th Division. A 3rd battalion of the Scots Guards was formed in late August 1914 and remained in the south of England throughout the war, training and shipping over 9,000 recruits to the 1st and 2nd battalions abroad. The Royal Scots Greys joined the 5th Cavalry Brigade within the Cavalry Division in 1914 and were in action by the 22nd of August. The seven regiments of Scottish Yeomanry remained at home until 1915, after which most sailed to Gallipoli, but A and B squadrons of the Glasgow Yeomanry and the Lothians and Border Horse had initial mounted service on the Western Front.

As the conflict mushroomed, so the organisation of the Army became steadily more complex and the Army itself grew inexorably larger and larger. The reforms in the decade or so before the outbreak of the war had gone a long way to prepare it for the inevitable trial of strength in Europe between the two alliances: Germany, Austria and – latterly – Turkey against Britain, France and Russia. By December 1914 the antagonists had given each other a terrible beating; British casualties in just five months were 80,000 – 40% of the Expeditionary Force. Without the Territorial Force, and without the New Armies raised by Kitchener, the war would – as so many people had predicted at its outset – have been over by Christmas, but with a British capitulation.

In the seven decades that have elapsed since the outbreak of the First World War more books have been written about all aspects of it than on any previous conflict. It was a characteristic of regimental histories written in the years between the wars, when many regimental histories were written, that the most recent conflict would occupy fully three-quarters of each book. The war and the part played in it by the regiment would be dealt with in exhaustive detail, always from the viewpoint of the commissioned ranks and frequently from a comparatively senior position. Brigade orders, battalion movements, platoon actions and even section assaults would figure in loving detail in a way that can only make one wish now that such treatment had been given to the earlier wars of the British Army. That such writing was possible was due largely to the enormous impact that the war had upon Britain and upon so many of its people. Few, probably none indeed, were left untouched by the war and it coloured their thinking for a quarter of a century in a way that explains much about the reaction of Britain at the end of the 1930s when another world conflict threatened. Even today, the battles fought between 1914 and 1918 have a power to induce the spinal shiver to an extent that no action of the Second World War possesses. Few now recall the true significance of Mons, or Le Cateau or the Marne or Loos but almost all have heard of the Somme, of Ypres – and particularly of the third battle of Ypres perhaps better known as Passchendaele. For so many, the First World War is represented by the trenches on the Western Front, a siege line from Switzerland to the sea; for slightly

115

Senior NCOs and men, 2nd battalion King's Own Scottish Borderers, Dublin 1914.

116

Signallers of 2nd battalion King's Own Scottish Borderers, Dublin 1914.

117

Machine-gun section, 2nd battalion King's Own Scottish Borderers, Dublin 1914.

118

Regimental tug-o-war team, 2nd battalion King's Own Scottish Borderers, Dublin 1914.

119

2nd battalion London Scottish drawn up for inspection in a London park.

less the awful waste of Gallipoli; for fewer still the campaign in Palestine and Egypt; and for virtually none the conflicts in Macedonia, Salonika and Africa. And that accounts only for the war on land. None of the theatres of war was without its Scottish contingent although in some, such as in South West Africa, the contingent was largely expatriate Scots: Transvaal Scottish and Capetown Highlanders.

At the most recent estimate, more than 147,000 soldiers of all ranks with a claim to be Scots sacrificed their lives during the war. Allowing a percentage for those expatriate Scots from Canada, South Africa and elsewhere in the Empire (the defence of which was supposedly the reason for their sacrifice), this means that just over a quarter of Scotland's males between the official age of 15 and 49 who enlisted never returned alive to their homeland. One in every four.

The experience varied from regiment to regiment. First across the Channel and last to retreat at Mons, the Argyll and Sutherland Highlanders eventually mustered 27 battalions; they lost nearly 7,000 men. The losses of the Cameron Highlanders were slightly higher out of their 11 battalions, one of which was dismounted yeomanry (The Lovat Scouts) and one Canadian (Queen's Own Cameron Highlanders of Canada). Of the King's Own Scottish Borderers 12 battalions, the first lost over half its strength on the killing ground of Y Beach at Gallipoli; its final butcher's bill came to over 6,800 men. The 2nd of an eventual 18 battalions of Royal Scots Fusiliers held the line at the first battle Ypres in 1914 for ten days and almost ceased to exist as a result; its losses comprised part of the

regiment's total of 5,800 dead. Largest both in terms of battalions raised and men lost was The Royal Scots; a phenomenal total of 35 battalions and a sickening one of 11,000 men killed. With three Canadian battalions and the dismounted Scottish Horse included in its total of 25 battalions, The Black Watch had more men killed than any other Highland regiment, just over 10,000. This figure was closely approached by The Gordon Highlanders who lost just over 9,000 soldiers from their 21 battalions. Of all Scottish infantry regiments, if they will pardon the description and association, the Scots Guards lost least soldiers during their time in France; from their two battalions 2,800 men died. The rapid stalemating of the war was an anticlimax for The Royal Scots Greys. After an initial time of true cavalry dash, the retreat to entrenched positions made the war one of frustration for them and, even in their periodic dismounted role, they lost only 154 men killed throughout the four years of war, scarcely more than at Waterloo in one afternoon. In addition to these Scotland-based regiments were the London, Liverpool and Tyneside Scottish, all of which formed several battalions within English regiments and, demonstrating varying degrees of Scottishness, amassed a sacrificial total of over 5,200.

The drain of the war, as battalion after battalion was fed into the mincing machine of Flanders, necessitated new forms of recruiting. The initial surge of patriotism, common throughout western Europe in 1914 in a way that is now both terrifying to consider and unbelievable, filled battalions as quickly as they could be formed. The New Armies

120

Divine Service in camp, The Royal Scots, about 1914.

which resulted were very different in composition to the ones which they relieved and, in many cases, replaced. There was increasingly more to it than patriotism however, as the serious decline in recruiting in the second half of 1915 showed. By then the seriously motivated recruits had all been used up and the numbers were slackening alarmingly despite repeated recruiting drives. It was this gradual drying-up which led to the introduction of conscription in January 1916, first for single men and, later in the year, for married men.

By the time that the first conscripts arrived in France, the remnants of the old Regular Army and those of the New Armies were, literally, dug in and well-used to the sort of life presented by the new type of warfare. The Army had survived the first two years of the war, just, and was rapidly learning lessons which would colour military thinking for several decades.

Steel helmets had begun to replace soft forage caps, Tam o'Shanters and Machine-Gun Corps except for a light machine-gun, the Lewis, which was found to be of consider-able tactical use to infantry sections. Uniforms had been modified to take account of conditions in the trenches and, on occasions when the kilt persisted, it would generally be worn under a wrap-around khaki cotton kilt-apron, with a pocket at the front to replace the sporran. Authorities dis-agree about the usefulness of the kilt in the trenches. Even though not all trenches were constantly knee-deep in water or liquid mud, as myth-perpetrators would have us believe, the kilt may well have had advantages over trousers or

breeches when they were worn since its use prevented the wearer from having to wear damp trousers. On the other hand, both kilt-wearers and their trousered compatriots both wore puttees and boots and these were the first things to get wet, so it has to be considered that stories of the advantages of the kilt in the trenches may have been much embroidered. The use of gas on the Western Front was an added inducement for kilt-wearers to don trousers; gas being no respecter of exposed skin. Soldiers continued to wear their heavy, hair khaki tunics, increasingly hung about with belts, bandoliers, blankets and other material necessary for survival. Officers wore knee-boots and breeches most of the time, except in Highland regiments when they too became ambivalent about the kilt, and, during advances across No-Man's Land, were conspicuous targets for German riflemen who learnt to identify them by the thinness of their knees and deal with them as a priority. The rubber gumboot, frequently mistakenly known as a Wellington boot, and the trenchcoat became current fashion for France and Flanders. In winter, sheepskin jerkins were worn by most ranks and particularly favoured by machine-gunners when in a static role. In theatres of war other than the Western Front, such as the Dardanelles, Egypt, Palestine or even Africa, clothing and weapons were again affected by the climate. Whereas in France and Flanders, covers were commonly used over the rifle mechanism to prevent it from becoming clogged with mud, in Gallipoli and other gener-ally dry and dusty climates similar measures were necessary to prevent the entrance of sand or dust into the complicated

121

Officers of the Royal Scots Greys, York, 1914.

bolt and magazine system. Outside the European theatre, the kilt was rapidly discarded in favour of shorts, usually khaki or (occasionally) tartan, or long trousers or breeches in order to protect the wearer from the attentions of insects attracted by the warmth of the more sensitive areas of the male anatomy. In sunny climates too the solar topi, or sun-helmet, was worn, now with a wider brim than that of the Boer War, and many soldiers adopted the slouch hat more usually associated with the Australian infantry. In all areas where the war was fought men did as they had always done and modified and adapted their kit and weapons to suit the exigencies of the environment. Rarely, it seems, had a British Army gone to war dressed and equipped suitably for the campaign that it was required to undertake: another of the unchanging facets of soldiering.

The raw materials of the Scottish regiments reflected a series of the differing layers of Scottish society throughout the war. In 1914 the structure of the regular battalions was marginally different from that of sixty years previously; those changes which had occurred in its social make-up were dealt with in the previous chapter. The Territorial battalions, as successors to the old Rifle Volunteers, remained similar socially to their predecessors: the ranks a slight cut above the Regular ranks, the officers a degree below their Regular peers. Such dangerous generalisations were destroyed in the first few months of the war and the formation of the New Armies hastened and completed the process. Recent surveys of the patterns of voluntary enlist-

ment after 4th August 1914 have revealed that, while patriotism cannot – and should not – be discounted as an explanation of the rush to the Colours, there were deeper and more underlying motives too. It might, though be observed that there can be no deeper motive than love for one's country.

Whatever the actual interpretations, there does seem to have been a genuine mass opinion that the war really would be over by Christmas. Lord Kitchener, Secretary of State for War, did not share this view (he had, as a young man, observed the terrible power of the Prussian Army in its victory over France in 1870). Large numbers of individuals, secure in this belief, joined up either so as not to miss what little war they believed there was going to be, or in order to be seen to be keen, assuming that it would all be over before they were sent abroad. The war rapidly induced a slump in some industries and this exacerbated the existing depression, which had led to widespread unemployment in manufacturing areas. The large numbers of unemployed now had an opportunity both to rectify their miserable states and perhaps gain a little honour in the process. In addition to these two categories of recruit there were those who joined up in order to avoid the privations which they felt the war would bring to the civilian population and those who felt it their duty to do so. This latter category were generally those who did not share the prevailing view of the war's early termination and were among the better-educated and employed members of society. As a rule, it appears,

122

Men of the 2nd Scots Guards and 2nd Gordon Highlanders in **SS Lake Michigan**, at Dover, 1914.

these individuals were not among the early recruits since they had affairs to set in order before presenting themselves at the recruiting offices. It is reasonably safe to assume that these recruits would be groomed for promotion, and even commissions, in their New Army battalions and, because of their relatively prosperous backgrounds, would probably not be among the 20% or so who were rejected from among potential recruits on health grounds before the end of 1914. Only once the best and most fit men had been butchered would the standards applied to recruits be lowered, in order to accept those weeded out on the grounds of health, age, or stature in the early months of the year.

The war and the need for cannon fodder encouraged the polarisation of social groups and this polarisation was exploited to the hilt by the agents of government who were charged with recruiting. Some examples of this had been seen with the Rifle Volunteer movement, where companies of similar individuals had been formed, and this was extended soon after the outbreak of war so that it transcended purely professional boundaries. Groups of people; workmates, school friends, members of working men's clubs, whole streets, all would be encouraged to enlist together and promised that they would serve together. Echoes of the methods of recruiting Highlanders in the late eighteenth century do not seem to have been noticed in Scotland. The battalions which came into evidence as a result of this exploitation of peer-groups were often known, principally in the Midlands and Northern England, as 'Pals'

battalions. Hundreds of young men who had grown up together enlisted together, and were to die together, leaving great gaps in the communities which they left out of a feeling of duty both to their country and to each other. In Scotland such battalions existed but do not seem to have employed the subtitle 'Pals' to themselves. It is possible that the attempt of Scots resident in Manchester to form a battalion might have resulted in it having such a soubriquet but, in the event, there were not enough of them and they were incorporated into the 15th battalion of The Royal Scots which had as its subtitle '1st City of Edinburgh': it was a pals battalion in all but name. So was The Royal Scots' 16th battalion; it took just thirteen days in October to come up to its strength of 1,350 men.

The 17th battalion of The Royal Scots demonstrated a uniformity, that it might now be thought patronising or distasteful to exploit. This was a Bantam battalion, recruited from men who were under the regulation height – itself lowered as the need for recruits pressed. With an average height of five feet, these Bantam battalions were rather despised by ones of more standard height but the 18th Highland Light Infantry had such a reputation for ferocity, even among the Glaswegians from which they sprang, that they bore the unofficial title of The Demon Dwarves. The extent to which people of 'normal' height tend to feel threatened, unaccountably, by people of small stature was regularly demonstrated throughout the war to the Bantam soldiers who, while developing a certain reputation for

123

2nd battalion Royal Scots Fusiliers in the trenches, Western Front. Winter 1914–15.

unruly behaviour, were often faster on their feet yet still ignored or belittled by their taller comrades. The propensity of intense industrial areas to produce men of small stature may explain why, alone of the Scottish regiments, two battalions of The Highland Light Infantry were Bantam battalions: the 18th, already mentioned, and the 14th, which absorbed the weeded-out remnant of a Cameronians Bantam battalion, the 13th, in February 1916.

Not all expatriate Scots battalions were the failure that the Manchester Scottish were. It may be that the Mancunians were fussy about the genealogical credentials of their recruits because, by not allowing such things to bother them overmuch, the Tyneside Scottish eventually recruited five battalions which, retaining a definably Scots identity despite not being uniformly Scots, were allied to the Northumberland Fusiliers.

Relics of the old profession-based recruiting remained, especially once the 1st New Army was recruited – largely from men not markedly dissimilar to the Regular Army's normal type of recruit. The 5th and 6th battalions of the Cameron Highlanders were fairly typical of the composition of the 2nd and 3rd New Armies in that they included companies recruited from the Glasgow Stock Exchange and University. These were men unlikely to be carried away by the enthusiasm of the early days and who were potentially giving up a lot to enlist. It is unlikely that they nourished any notion of being home by Christmas.

Unlike the Territorial Force battalions, which were contracted only to serve at home (a condition which volunteering for service overseas soon breached), the New Army battalions were committed to overseas service. Although the headquarters of many battalions remained at home for the entire war, their function was to oversee the processing and transmission of soldiers abroad once they had been trained. The home service force which existed during the war manifested itself as a form of early Home Guard called, generically, the Volunteer Training Corps. The few Scottish units of the Corps were principally based in central and southern Scotland. The Perthshire and Fife Volunteer Regiments were eventually being organised to form the 5th to 9th Volunteer Battalions of the Black Watch. The Dumfries-shire Volunteer Regiment became the 3rd Volunteer Battalion of The King's Own Scottish Borderers. While fulfilling certain of the functions of the later Home Guard the force acted primarily as a training cadre for volunteers into the Army.

The war involved the whole British Empire and, because decisions made in London affected the Dominions and colonies as much as they affected Britain, when Britain went to war so did Canada, Australia, New Zealand, South Africa, India and all the other territories scattered across the globe which owed allegiance to The King-Emperor. Each of the colonies, territories or Dominions participated to an extent in the war and many demonstrated, yet again, the

125

Men of 6th battalion Argyll and Sutherland Highlanders dug in near Ypres.

126

127

Captain L.D. Ranken, Seaforth Highlanders, shaving in
camp in France 1915.

Men of 1st battalion Seaforth Highlanders in a reserve trench
behind the front line, France 1915.

128

First type of gas mask issued to the 2nd battalion Argyll and Sutherland Highlanders 1915.

131

14 Platoon, D Company, 7th (Leith) battalion The Royal Scots, April 1915. Of D. Company, only two men survived the Gretna rail crash of May 1915.

Officers of the 51st (Highland) Division at the Machine-Gun School, Ripon, about 1916.

capacity for a Scottish element to become revealed. This was largest by far from Canada, where Scots had been settling and retaining (or even enlarging) their sense of identity for well over a century by 1914. The Canadian regiments, regular and militia, in 1914 represented a formidable presence and were formed into the Canadian Expeditionary Force which eventually comprised four divisions in which over 400,000 Canadians served and over 60,000 died.

Of the battalions of the Canadian Expeditionary Force, 56 were later to become Canadian Scottish regiments and many of that number already claimed a degree of association with Scotland long before the events of 1914 claimed Canada's young men in such quantities. The Black Watch of Canada, for instance, began life in 1862, raised the 13th, 42nd and 73rd battalions of the Expeditionary Force in 1914 and were to include three winners of the Victoria Cross before the end of hostilities. Via various changes of title, they had been conspicuously Scots since 1880. The Highland Light Infantry of Canada recruited three battalions for France in 1914 and adopted its Scottish affiliation a year later. There were many more Canadian Scottish regiments and their contribution to the First World War was considerable.

Many of the battalions of the Australian and New Zealand Army Corps that were blooded at Gallipoli had been formed from militia or volunteer units which claimed Scottish associations but had been forced to adopt the anonymity of numbers as part of the Australian Imperial Forces. Even in Shanghai in 1914 a company of the Shanghai Defence Force was raised from expatriate Scots, adopted Hunting Stewart kilts and paraded regularly to maintain a semblance of law and order in that far-away outpost of the Empire.

Closer to home, however, things were rather more realistic. By the middle of 1915 the 'Home by Christmas' spirit was rapidly dispersing and the Army on the Western Front settling itself for a long slow haul. Almost as if the daily deaths and periodic carnage on the Western Front were not enough, the 7th battalion of The Royal Scots, entrained for France, were caught in an enormous train crash just north of Gretna in May 1915. The train they were packed into like sardines thundered into a local train containing civilians and then the joint wreckage of those two trains was run into at high speed by a Glasgow-bound express with two engines at the front. The slaughter was frightful and worsened by the fact that the wooden carriages caught fire and burnt fiercely. Of 470 men of the battalion, only 58 were able to answer their names at a roll-call; 200 died, along with 50 civilians.

Such devastation was little compared to what was waiting for the Army at Loos in September 1915. After a month's fighting, 50,000 men were dead, 15,000 of whom were never found. In the 5th battalion of the Cameron Highlanders only 112 men were left out of the 850 who had withstood the

95

Gully bombing post. Ypres Salient, 1916.

gas and shelling before fixing bayonets and climbing up the ladders into history. The King's Own Scottish Borderers were encouraged in the face of an artillery bombardment and clouds of gas by Piper Laidlaw who played them forward under an incessant bombardment. How much of 'All the Blue Bonnets are over the Border' was audible is not recorded but Laidlaw received a Victoria Cross for his trouble. The 1st Seaforth Highlanders and 2nd Black Watch went to Mesopotamia after Loos and, in operations against the Turks, were so reduced in numbers that for a time they were regimented together.

The war dragged on for three more years after Loos in a series of advances, stalemates, withdrawals and more advances until the collapse of Germany internally and the eventual effects of the blockade brought the greatest war that the world had ever known to a close. Trumpeted as the War to End All Wars and commemorated on one of its campaign medals as The Great War for Civilization, it is a war that renders statistics meaningless and cannot but sicken by its apparent waste of human life. Such, to a greater or lesser extent, are all wars. Britain's total casualties were far less than those of France, or Russia or Germany but, as was noted at the beginning of this chapter, Scotland's contribution was considerable, relative to her population size.

It was a war which changed much about people's concepts of things. Little was left untouched or unaffected and nothing would ever be the same again. Although it took another ten years for all women to be given the vote in Britain, there is no doubt that their contribution to the war hastened the process. Women became involved with the Armed Forces to a far closer extent than ever before, as nurses and as uniformed auxiliaries. The First Aid Nursing Yeomanry provided nurses as well as ambulance drivers; Queen Mary's Auxiliary Army Corps provided essential back-up behind the lines; the Scottish Women's Hospitals, funded by voluntary contributions which totalled nearly £½ million by the end of the war, provided hospital services in conjunction with the Red Cross wherever the war was waged.

The Scottish regiments were bigger than they ever had been and although, by the end of the war, many had been split up and were not serving in any of the Divisions with Scottish sub-titles, those Divisions retained a conspicuously Scottish identity until peace necessitated their disbandment. The anonymity that the standardisation of the Army required during the war meant that there was little, other than the use of the kilt, the Tam o'Shanter or glengarry, which differentiated the Scottish soldier from any other soldier. Soldiers generally look the same when caked with mud or reddened with dust and war is no respecter of nationalities. Scots enlisted for the usual variety of reasons, fought, lived, died, existed in the squalor of the trenches or the dust of Mesopotamia and, eventually, all that was left of them came home. There were few towns that were without their victory parade: soldiers in their best khaki, glengarries or Tam o'Shanters, trews or kilts, the ubiquitous pipers and the in-

134

Evacuating the wounded from a communication trench in Salonika. London Scottish, 1916.

evitable tears. It is doubtful whether there is one community in Scotland that is without its war memorial and there can have been few families untouched by bereavement.

There was no way of telling, in 1918, that the war just ended would inevitably lead to another two decades later and as those Scots who came home handed in their rifles and put away their uniforms they must have felt that their achievement and their comrades' sacrifice had been worthwhile. Those who still had jobs (or were physically sound enough to rebuild their lives by getting them) were the lucky ones. For many Scots there continued to be little alternative to going for a soldier.

135

12th Argyll & Sutherland Highlanders, Salonika, 1916.

138

Officer's mess tent, 1st battalion Seaforth Highlanders, Mesopotamia, 1917.

139

137

Seaforth Highlanders manning a trench-periscope, Mesopotamia, 1916.

Soldiers of 1st battalion Seaforth Highlanders resting in trenches, Mesopotamia 1916.

140

A group of officers of the 1st battalion Seaforth Highlanders, all of whom rose from the ranks during the war and two of whom commanded battalions by its end. Mesopotamia.

141

No 7 Light Car Patrol (Scottish Horse), Egyptian Expeditionary Force, Mesopotamia, 1917.

Kit inspection, Scots Guards, Wellington Barracks, about 1917.

Pipes and drums of the 2nd battalion, Seaforth Highlanders, in France, 1918.

143B

Battle of the Scarpe. Men of the 6th Seaforth Highlanders working their way towards Delbar Wood, North East of Roeux. 1918

143C

Patrol of the 6th Seaforth Highlanders entering a German dug-out. 1918.

CHAPTER EIGHT

BRASSES, BLANCO AND BULL

1918 to 1939

It is clear, from the haste with which the Army returned to its pre-1914 attitudes, that it – as a whole – had not enjoyed the changes which the war had forced upon it. More than one officer is recorded as indicating his relief at the prospect of peace-time soldiering and it is likely that this view was not uncommon among non-commissioned ranks too. For the bulk of the 1918 Army, hastily-recruited conscripts, the chief priority was to get out of uniform and back to civilian life as soon as possible.

Unfortunately, things were not quite so simple. The actual business of demobilising an Army of over a million men, spread across the globe but concentrated just across the Channel or straining at the leash at home, was far more complicated in 1918 than it ever had been. People's expectations had been changed by the four previous years and military administration become more complex without simplifying the actual mechanics of turning soldiers back into civilians. Much as it would probably have liked to have done, government could not just claim back equipment and turn the soldier onto the street as had been the practice after previous wars. Affecting the business of demobilisation too was the genuine fear of Bolshevik-inspired subversion among discontented (and armed) soldiers with no identifiable enemy against whom to be directed. There was also an election looming and Germany, rapidly falling apart from inside, had to be occupied in order to see that she honoured the terms of the Armistice. Aside from spectral Bolsheviks at home there were also real ones in Russia and those required attention too, so did a renewed Afghan nuisance on the North-West Frontier of India. Ireland was about to dissolve into fratricidal chaos, yet again, and the relinquished German colonies all required their new administrations to be propped up by at least token military presences. Britain had wider and larger worldwide commitments than ever and, with a government anxious to reduce military expenditure and an Army that just wanted to go home, such forces as were left were going, necessarily, to be spread transparently thin.

Scotland's total losses from the war represented approximately one-fifth of Britain's dead. Apart from being a nation of widows and fatherless children, she also had a National Hero on her hands. Douglas Haig, never the most approachable of men, now found himself loaded with honours and credited with the victory. Not until after his death did the disquiet about the actual cost of the victory, in terms of lives, manifest itself in a growing literature which eventually came seriously to question the tactics employed in defeating Germany. This literature, ranging from impenetrable war histories through self-justifying memoirs to popular novels, was gradually to establish the figure of Haig The Butcher and the apparently unshakeable belief in what passes for the popular consciousness that all the First World War generals were port-sodden incompetents who knew little and cared less for the lives of the men at the Front. As the BEF's senior soldier from late 1915, when he replaced that other misinterpreted cavalryman, Sir John French, Haig naturally attracted his fair share of calumny. Although partially rehabilitated in recent years, his name still represents uncaring slaughter for far too many people. Whatever the truth of the matter, his foundation of the Royal British Legion in 1921 and constant attention to its affairs until his death seven years later must count for much more than just a guilty conscience.

Operations in Russia against the Bolshevik Red Armies occupied various Scottish units during 1918 and 1919 until the cause was realised as lost (and long-term damage to relations between Britain and the Soviet government ensured). Detachments of The Royal Scots, 2nd Royal Scots Fusiliers, 2nd Highland Light Infantry and 2nd Cameron Highlanders fought alongside White Russian troops in northern and southern Russia during the period.

The crushing of the Easter Rising in Dublin in 1916, culminating in the martyrdom of most of its leaders, had done little to settle the condition of Ireland and operations were carried on between 1918 and 1922 against units of the Irish Republican Army which involved, amongst others, 1st Royal Scots Fusiliers, 1st and 2nd Cameronians and 2nd Argyll and Sutherland Highlanders. Although the partition of Ireland momentarily settled part of the question in 1922, and resulted in the disbandment of five Irish infantry regiments, Irishmen from the south of Ireland continued to cross the water to enlist in the British Army. Decreasingly though, their names appeared in the rolls of Scottish regiments.

Imperial policing characterised the operations of the British Army during the 1920s and '30s and Scottish units and Scots soldiers served wherever the map was coloured pink – and in many places where it wasn't.

The relinquishing of colonies by the defeated Central Powers had resulted in them being governed by mandate from the newly-created, and persistently sickly, League of Nations. Prominent among these territories was Palestine, which became increasingly a centre for conflict throughout the period between the wars. By the 1930s, when it was seen as a refuge for Jews fleeing persecution in central Europe, this territory, along with the North-West Frontier, re-presented the biggest area of commitment for the Army during the period under review.

The obsession with India, which had not slackened with the replacement of Czarist Russia by Soviet Russia, per-sisted throughout the 1920s and '30s. Allied to the supposed Russian threat from the north, was a perceived growing menace from the east – in the shape of Japan – and burgeoning movements for independence within. It was recognised by 1931 that India would eventually become

144

Captain Tyringham and Lieutenants Harvey and Mayfield, King's Guard, St James's Palace, 1923.

Below: Scots Guards practising for The King's Birthday Parade, 1923.

145

The Prince of Wales and the Viceroy of India inspect 2nd battalion Seaforth Highlanders, India, 1923.

146

Officers of 1st battalion The Royal Scots, Secunderabad.

147

148

Pipes and drums, 1st battalion The Cameronians (Scottish Rifles), at the Tower of London, about 1923.

independent and the granting of Dominion status in that year put her on the same footing – at least in theory – as Canada and Australia. Giving in to demands for self-determination and the gradual 'Indianisation' of the Indian Army did not reduce the persistent nuisance of Afghanistan however and, four times between the ending of one war and the beginning of the next, detachments of Scottish regiments were engaged on the Frontier. Men of The Highland Light Infantry and Seaforth and Gordon Highlanders were there during the Third Afghan War of 1919, probably as machine-gun or signalling sections. The 2nd Seaforth Highlanders were there in strength in 1930 and 1931 and four years later the 2nd Argyll and Sutherland Highlanders were also getting their knees brown. The Argylls were rejoined by the Highland Light Infantry for the Frontier campaign of 1936–37.

All the Scottish regiments served East of Suez between the wars as, while old regimes were replaced by new ones, crisis after crisis threatened British interests or residents on the fringes of the Empire. The Mediterranean, China, the Sudan, Burma and Singapore each heard the sound of the bagpipes at various times. Despite, however, the important policing role of the Army, the wide spread of Empire and the persistence of traditional concepts, together with the overestimated potential of new ones, led increasingly to the Army coming third in priority to the needs of the Royal Navy and Royal Air Force and, throughout the period from 1923 until 1932 the Army was reduced in size and spending

power. It was felt that what the Royal Navy could not bombard, the Royal Air Force could bomb. The role of the Army became less well-defined than ever and, rather than re-treating to the position of 1914, when it was at least trained, equipped and, other than in its size, prepared for a European land war, it – if anything – resumed the attitudes of the 1890s, when it was ready for little except small colonial wars (occasionally) and immaculate parades (regularly).

Allied to the parsimonious attitude of government, which – from 1919 – annually renewed what became known as the Ten Year Rule (that Britain would not be required to fight a major European war within ten years), was the national feeling of both complacency at the victory of 1918 and revul-sion at the sacrifice which it had necessitated. Complacency, especially with an Empire that was bigger than ever (even if it was coming apart at the seams), allowed the neglect of the Army's fighting potential, of which few civilians are every fully aware anyway. Revulsion, national guilt, shame or sad-ness, combined with the creation of multitudes of war memorials to produce, in most parts of the country, a more negative attitude than ever to soldiering. Even the post-war slump and the Depression of the late '20s and early '30s did not bring in to the Army the recruits that it needed. In any case, between 1923 and 1932 its numbers were forced down-wards by government so that large-scale recruiting drives – which would have been unsuccessful in the main anyway – were not encouraged.

149

Pipe-Majors and Drum-Majors of the Scottish regiments, about 1923.

Such recruitment as there was was, of course and as usual, affected by such matters as pay and conditions. The soldier's pay had been doubled in 1919 from that which he had received in 1914. By 1923 he was paid, on average, one pound, seventeen shillings and three pence (£1.86) per week, a sum that was reduced in 1925 to one pound, twelve shillings (£1.60). The figures quoted include amounts allowed for his food and accommodation and not actually paid to him at the end of each week. In real, and average, terms the soldier of 1925 received two shillings (10p) per day. In 1937, in the face of mounting national concern at the activities in Germany (once again) and as part of rapidly-implemented reforms and improvements in the Army, the pay of the private soldier was increased to three shillings (15p) per day, after three years' service. Conditions, at home and abroad, reverted to pre-1914 with a vengeance and were most noticeable in factors such as discipline and dress.

This was the Army of polished brasses, immaculate webbing belts and a smartness of appearance and turnout which must, for many non-commissioned officers – probably consciously, have represented a reaction to the squalor of wartime conditions and the laxity enforced, in most regiments, by the impossibility of keeping kit and body clean. Although officers had retained their full-dress uniforms for special occasions, the scarlet coat had gone for good for the soldiers of line infantry regiments, except in the bands, and much effort was expended in making the khaki service dress uniform of tunic, breeches and puttees as smart

as possible – a complete contradiction of its original function. Scots retained their kilts and sporrans, or trews, throughout the period between the wars and although Battledress, that most deliberately unsmart of fighting uniforms, was adopted in 1937, many Scots marched off to war two years later in the khaki service dress worn – tailored, polished and with razor-sharp creases – since 1902.

Barrack-room life continued much the same as before the war, in the gradually more civilized barracks and garrisons created during the first decades of the twentieth century. Officers' lives were centred around varying degrees of training and leisure, both pastimes depending upon the locality of their posting, and although greater attention was paid to the welfare and health of of the other ranks, there was a lot of concentration on the minutiae of maintaining smartness and drill. There is some evidence to suggest that the consumption of alochol in garrison canteens gradually slackened during the period. If this is so, it may be associated with a better quality of recruit produced by a combination of less as a whole coming forward and the Army's gradually tighter selection procedure. Although it is certain that recruits continued to come from the same stratas of society that had always provided them, an increase in the standard of living outside the Army and tighter administration of the ranks within, together with better education and medical skills, combined to make the lot of the enlisted soldier less dependent upon alcohol than heretofore. Scotland suffered from chronic unemployment and resultant

Walking Out Order	Musketry Order	Ceremonial Order	Fatigue Dress	Marching Order	Full Dress (Drummer)	Full Dress (Piper)

Full Dress (Pipe Major)	Full Dress (Bandsman)	Fighting Order	Blue Patrol Dress	Drill Order	Ceremonial Order (Piper)	Full Dress (Drum Major)

Orders of dress for other ranks, 2nd battalion, The Royal Scots, 1924.

152

| Undress Order (Galloway) | Full Dress (Gray) | Drill Order (Crockatt) | Undress Order Mounted Officer (Col. L.K. Smith) | Fighting Order (Mitchell Innes) Marching Order includes a slung waterproof | Ceremonial Order C.O., 2nd in Com'd, Adjt (Hall) | Ceremonial Order (Coutts) | Blue Patrol Order (Robertson-Glasgow) |

Orders of dress for officers, 2nd battalion, The Royal Scots, 1924.

widespread poverty in the '20s and '30s but, because the Army was less able to absorb large numbers of recruits and more choosy about the phsyical and educational standards of those that it did accept, the condition of Scotland did not result, markedly, in more Scots serving in the Army during the period; a reversal of what was once the case for similar reasons.

The sacrifice of Britain's young men, and women, was keenly felt throughout the years between the wars. For some this sacrifice produced pacifism and, eventually, appeasement. For others, generally the leaders of society, it meant commemoration. In national terms this commemoration took two forms: memorials and museums. The British Empire was the only one of the combatants to institute museums to commemorate the war and these still exist in present and past Commonwealth countries: The Imperial War Museum in London; the Australian National War Memorial in Canberra; the Canadian War Museum in Ottowa; the South African National War Museum in Johannesburg; the Scottish United Services Museum in Edinburgh Castle. Each of these was founded in the years between the wars and each, with the significant exception of the last, employs the word 'War' in its title. In England memorials were exemplified by the Cenotaph in Whitehall, in Scotland

by the Scottish National War Memorial in Edinburgh Castle. This latter memorial was created from an old barrack block and opened in 1927; its foundation led to the founding, three years later, of Scotland's national military museum. Both institutions are a direct reflection of the way in which Scotland wished to commemorate its sacrifice during the war and the Memorial itself, which is deliberately more personal than the (equally deliberately) impersonal Cenotaph, still retains the power to move even the most cynical of visitor.

The Army of occupation left the Rhineland in 1930 and, two years later, the size of the Army as a whole was 207,000 men. During the 1930s it served principally in the Middle and Far East when it wasn't at home. The Ten Year Rule was not renewed after 1932 but the Army remained resolutely backward for several more years after that. Even once the threat from a Germany infected by Nazism had been appreciated, after 1934, the Army remained subordinated to the other two services in terms of the amount allowed for its modernisation and rearmament. Even the little money that it did get was not well spent, in view of the type of war that was unleashed upon it in 1940, but this – of course – is easily seen with the comfortable benefit of hindsight. Because of a belief in the destructive power of airstrikes and a lack of understanding of the potential presented by a combination of tanks, mechanised infantry and supporting air-power, priority was given to anti-aircraft expenditure, to the construction of a rapidly-obsolescent bomber fleet and to the building of light tanks (which were fine for police actions against Pathan villages but of little use in massed formations against heavier-gunned adversaries). Army tactics were debated *ad nauseam* throughout the '20s and '30s and the dual, or separate, roles of, first, tanks and infantry and, then, the Army and the Royal Air Force presented in a variety of ways. The result, by 1937, was that no solution had really been found (other than increasing the numbers of conventional forces and, one suspects, hoping that it Would Never Happen). In any case, the whole reasoning behind Cabinet-inspired military strategy was not that attack was the best form of defence but rather that, in the event of a war, Britain would prepare herself for defence rather than equip herself for attack; hence searchlight and anti-aircraft batteries rather than fleets of medium or heavy tanks.

National lack of interest in the Armed Services had affected the Territorials too and, although the Territorial Army – created from the Territorial Force in 1921 – remained in being throughout the period, its position was weakened in real terms by lack of governmental encouragement.

All this began to change in 1937 when Leslie Hore-Belisha became Secretary of State for War in Neville Chamberlain's government. Wide-ranging reforms were introduced into the Army in order to drag it into the realities of the late '30s. As we have seen, pay was made more competitive and uniforms more functional. Conditions of service, barracks and cooking all improved and recruitment was actively increased. The Cabinet, strongly influenced by Chamberlain, resisted all attempts at large-scale expansion of the Army until German forces occupied Prague and annexed the remaining unswallowed portion of Czechoslovakia early in 1939. It was then realised, five years too late, that the Army only recently allowed to equip five Regular and four Territorial Divisions for a war in Europe would be grossly inadequate, even with the eventual, and grudging, back-up of seven other Divisions. At the end of March 1939 the Territorial Army was ordered to be doubled in size and a month later conscription was reintroduced.

Echoes of 1914 in 1939 do not ring true. The British Expeditionary Force of 1939 was small, ill-trained and even more unprepared for what it was to confront than that of 1914 which, though small, was superbly trained and equipped though not, again, for the type of war that transpired.

The Scottish Regular soldier of 1939 was of a higher quality than his predecessor a quarter of a century earlier. Although he was wearing almost the same uniform and armed with much the same weapons, he was likely to be fitter, better fed, certainly better paid and probably better educated than the Regular of his father's generation. It is likely that his only experience of recent active service would have been either on the Frontier or in Palestine, where eight battalions of Scottish infantry, and the Scots Greys, served in the late '30s. For the next six years he would be largely indistinguishable from other British soldiers in his ill-fitting battledress and steel helmet. Principal among the differences between the Scottish soldier of 1939 and his predecessor a generation before was that the soldier of 1939 was less likely to be there for reasons of enthusiastic patriotism, but rather ones of resigned determination. Few, too, nurtured the belief that, this time, it would all be over by Christmas.

153

Scots Guards piper in service dress, about 1928.

110

Officers of the Royal Scots Greys in Meerut, India, 1926.

154

155

Guard of Honour, Royal Scots Fusiliers, at the Royal Tournament 1928.

156

London Scottish forming part of Lord Haig's funeral procession, Horse Guards Building, London 1928.

157

Major J.C.O. Marriott, Scots Guards, 1930.

158

Lieutenant-Colonel J.E. Lawrie DSO and Major-General Sir Archibald Ritchie KBE CB
CMG, 2nd Seaforth Highlanders, on their way to attend a levée at St James's Palace,
London, 1935.

159

Pipe-Major and pipers, 2nd battalion The Cameronians (Scottish Rifles), 1935.

160

The Adjutant of 1st battalion The Royal Scots, Lieutenant A.G. Mackenzie-Kennedy, inspecting the Royal Stewart pipe ribbons bestowed upon the regiment to celebrate its tercentenary, 1933.

114

Regimental Association Football team, Royal Scots Greys, 1936 Runners-up in the Cavalry Cup Final.

161

162

163

A private of The Highland Light Infantry in full marching order, about 1936.

A warrant officer of The Highland Light Infantry, about 1938.

164

Cooks of King's Own Scottish Borderers.

165

King's Own Scottish Borderers at 11 o'clock tea.

166

Royal Scots Greys exercising their mounts.

167

Officers of the 2nd battalion The Cameronians
(Scottish Rifles).

168

Bren Gun on anti-aircraft mounting manned by Scots Guards.

CHAPTER NINE

TOTAL WAR

1939 to 1945

For some time before the London air-raid sirens coincided significantly with the ending of the Prime Minister's wireless broadcast, preparations had been under way to create the nucleus of a British Expeditionary Force that would cross the Channel quickly and form up on the flank of the French. Resignation tinged with complacency seemed to be the order of the day. The French had the Maginot Line, we had the Royal Navy – which would rapidly blockade Germany into submission – and in any case, the German economy was on its last legs. Any actual concerns seemed to be principally fear of air attacks, possibly involving gas, and so, as the children continued to vanish into the silence of the country-side, the gas mask (or at least its container) became part of daily wear. There was no rush to the Colours as there had been a quarter of a century before, just an orderly calling-up of reserves and gradual implementation of conscription. The Territorial Army became absorbed into the Regular Army, kilts were returned to store – except by pipers who generally managed to conceal theirs somewhere, and a largely Battle-dressed army crossed the Channel in stages starting shortly after the beginning of the war.

Scottish regiments were spread throughout the British Expeditionary Force. Initially, 1st and 2nd Army Corps crossed the Channel. 1st Corps contained 6th Gordon Highlanders as part of the 2nd Infantry Brigade within the 1st Division, together with 1st Royal Scots and 1st Cameron Highlanders as part, respectively, of 4th and 5th Infantry Brigades within the 2nd Division. 1st King's Own Scottish Borderers were part of the 9th Infantry Brigade within the 3rd Division of 2nd Corps, and 6th Black Watch formed part of 12th Infantry Brigade in the 4th Division of the same Corps.

It was to be another war of the large formations and, even more than in the First World War, with the submerging of regimental identities under steel helmets, loyalties quickly sprang up to Brigades or Divisions to join those already held to regiments. In some cases, as men were despatched, drafted and cross-posted within and between large formations, to regiments of which they had occasionally never even heard, Divisional loyalties replaced regimental ones. In any case, with war on the grand scale, little was achievable at purely regimental strength.

By the time that the German Army was ready, in the face of deliberate non-provocation by the British and French, to turn *sitzkrieg* into *blitzkrieg*, the Scottish component of the British Expeditionary Force numbered twenty-eight battalions, including a battalion of Tyneside Scottish (who were brigaded with 10th and 11th Durham Light Infantry in a move that owed more to geographical factors than national-istic ones). The concentration of Scottish battalions was in 51st (Highland) Division and 52nd (Lowland) Division, both Territorial Divisions, like their predecessors with the same numbers in the First World War. The 52nd landed after the tanks and Stukas had begun to roll up the French and British armies and had to make a fighting withdrawal to Cherbourg, where they had landed, in order to disembark. The 157th Brigade of the 52nd, comprising 1st Glasgow Highlanders (formerly the only kilted battalion of the Highland Light Infantry) and 5th and 6th Highland Light Infantry covered the withdrawal, with 5th King's Own Scottish Borderers scampering in at the last moment to disembark when the German Army was little more than three miles from the harbour.

The 51st (Highland) Division was less fortunate. Landing at Le Havre in January 1940, it eventually comprised 1st and 4th Black Watch, 2nd and 4th Seaforth Highlanders, 1st and 5th Gordon Highlanders, 4th Cameron Highlanders and 7th and 8th Argyll and Sutherland Highlanders within three Infantry Brigades. The regular battalions of the Black Watch, Seaforth and Gordon Highlanders replaced the 6th battalions of their regiments in March in order, it was felt, to stiffen what was otherwise a wholly Territorial, and there-fore undertrained, Division. At first, the Divisional Cavalry had been formed by 1st Fife and Forfar Yeomanry but these were later replaced by 1st Lothians and Border Horse. Throughout the gradually-reducing period of uncertainty known as the 'Phoney War' the Division strengthened defences, with the aid of the 6th (Pioneer) Royal Scots Fusiliers, in the Saar sector and awaited developments. These were not long in coming and the German attack in May forced the Division eventually to retire upon Abbeville in alliance with the French 9th Army. Here they formed a thin defensive line but were gradually forced westward by a German force much superior in numbers, with undisputed command of the air and no enemies behind them once the original BEF had been evacuated at Dunkirk. From that

170

Scots Guards Guard of Honour for HM King George VI at Caledonian Station, Edinburgh, 1939.

point it was retirement all the way as the Division was forced back west, then encircled from the south, and given no option but to retreat within a tightening ring of armour and infantry upon the coastal town of St. Valéry-en-Caux. Some troops were disembarked before the port was made indefensible by bombardment but eventually the Division surrendered on 12th June, having suffered heavy casualties.

The Division was resurrected in Britain very rapidly from the 9th (Scottish) Division, which was renumbered 51st and the regular Highland battalions re-raised. Thereafter, for the next eighteen months or so, like most Divisions not active overseas, the 51st went into intensive training, with Divisional and Brigade headquarters based in the north-east of Scotland.

The duplication of the Territorial Army in the spring of 1939 had resulted in the creation of 15th (Scottish) Division from 52nd (Lowland) Division by the time that war broke out in September and its various headquarters were scattered around central and southern Scotland. The 44th Brigade was centred in the Lothians area, the 45th around Hamilton and the 46th in Glasgow. As matters became more organised by the end of September the Division as a whole moved into the Borders and the Brigades were based on the Border towns; the 44th in Melrose, St. Boswells and Earlston, the 45th in Hawick and the 46th in Galashiels. The Divisional artillery was based in Selkirk and, with Divisional headquarters, in Jedburgh. During the Phoney War period the Division changed camps in Scotland regularly, forming part of the defences of the Forth and Clyde through the winter of 1939. The Division left Scotland for southern England in the late spring of 1940 and, when the breakthrough of the Germany Army in France occurred in May 1940, it became part of the defensive forces ranged along the south coast.

The nature of Divisional organisation was far more than just a collection of infantry battalions or armoured regiments. Each Division had its own supporting arms such as artillery, engineers, signals, companies of the Royal Army Service Corps and Field Ambulance sections of the Royal Army Medical Corps. Therefore, whereas on its foundation the 15th Division had nine battalions of Territorial Infantry ranged among its three Infantry Brigades, it also had three field regiments and one anti-tank regiment of Royal Artillery Territorials, three Field Companies and one Field Park Company of Royal Engineer Territorials, a signals section, three companies of Service Corps and three Field Ambulance sections as well as a Field Hygiene Section of the Medical Corps. The Order of Battle of all Divisions became steadily more complex as the war progressed but they, and the Army as a whole, had one thing principally in common; they were gradually composed more and more of soldiers created out of conscripted civilians.

For Britain, the Second World War was a conscripts' war even more than the First World War had been. The BEF of 1939 and 1940 had been largely composed, like its predecessor of 1914, of Regular and Territorial battalions. Many of these were among the 4,438 killed, 14,127 wounded and 39,251 made prisoner before the remaining 200,000 could be

171

172

Soldiers of the Gordon Highlanders en route to
Aberdeen railway station to join the BEF for
France 1939.

Pipes and drums of the Seaforth Highlanders and Cameron Highlanders lead a draft of
trained recruits out of Fort George, about 1940.

taken off the Dunkirk beaches. The defeat of the BEF in
1940 was similar to its destruction at Mons, Le Cateau and
1st Ypres in the opening months of the First World War
inasmuch as it presented Britain with a real chance of
actually losing the war quite quickly. In both cases, German
failure or inability to capitalise on early success, together
with British armies formed from non-soldiers, combined
with other factors to avert a catastrophe. The conscripts of
the Second World War were different in many ways from
those of 1916 and onwards. The setting of the precedent of
conscription in 1916 had made it easy for government to
renew it in 1939 (most people forgot, if they had ever
known, that the wars against Napoleon had involved a type
of conscription). The years between the wars had been ones
of revulsion at militarism, ones of the development of the
cinema, the wireless, television, motor cars for many of the
population and improved health and education. People's
expectations had advanced and their horizons broadened
from those of the pre-1914 generations and, although for
many the '20s and '30s had been decades of unemployment,
depression and industrial unrest, the conscripts who were
called up after 1939 came from a very different world to
those summoned a generation earlier. The Army (and
indeed the other two services) had to appreciate this fact
and, difficult though it undoubtedly was – especially at first
with a cadre of pre-war, spit-and-polish NCOs, adjust their
thinking about training, discipline and use of manpower
accordingly. Armies composed of large formations could ill-
afford, especially in time of national crisis, to pay too much

attention to the cultural background of their recruits and so
large blocks of men might easily find themselves serving
alongside other groups with whom they had nothing in
common. This certainly occurred in the various Scottish
Divisions and happened to large numbers of Scots who
found themselves serving in non-Scottish Divisions. The persistent national character of the Scottish Divisions,
however, especially in the 51st after its reraising and
command by that ultra-Scot Douglas Wimberley, was
notable for its ability to transform non-Scots into being
more Scottish than their native Scot comrades. Or so
Scottish historians of Scottish Divisions would have us
believe.

Occasionally a fortunate, though probably not coin-
cidental, inclusion of a Scottish unit would occur in an
Infantry Division, such as when 54th (Queen's Own Royal
Glasgow Yeomanry) Anti-Tank Regiment, Royal Artillery
became part of 52nd (Lowland) Division in 1939. Few of the
Scottish Yeomanry regiments retained their cavalry function
during the war and most were converted to units of the
Royal Artillery with various specialist roles.

Only the Fife and Forfar Yeomanry and the Lothians and
Border Horse remained as cavalry units and each comprised
two armoured regiments within Armoured Divisions. As
had been mentioned above, the 1st Fife and Forfar and 1st
Lothians and Border went to France in 1940, were briefly
associated with 51st (Highland) Division and escaped at
Dunkirk without their hardware. 1st Fife and Forfar formed
part of 9th Armoured Division until moving to 79th

Recruits in denim overalls at rifle drill, Fort George, about 1940.

Armoured Division prior to the invasion of Europe in 1944 when they were re-equipped with 'Crocodiles' – flame-thrower tanks. 2nd Fife and Forfar joined 11th Armoured Division and swept across northern Europe after D-Day, finishing up at Lübeck in northern Germany by the end of the war. After Dunkirk 1st Lothians and Border Horse reformed and went back after D-Day eventually to fight their way through Holland and Germany. 2nd Lothians and Border Horse went to North Africa in 1942, fought across the Western Desert, invaded Italy in 1943 and were present at the Battle of Monte Cassino.

With the exception of the Lovat Scouts, all the other Scottish Yeomanry regiments relinquished the vestiges of their cavalry function and took over those of artillery. The Lovat Scouts were converted into a mountain reconnaissance unit after brief service in the Faeroe Islands and training in Canada and fought as specialist troops in Italy after 1944. The Ayrshire Yeomanry formed 151st and 152nd Field Regiments, Royal Artillery; 151st being included in the invasion of Europe and 152nd crossing North Africa and joining the attack on Italy. The Lanarkshire Yeomanry turned into 155th and 156th Field Regiments; most of 155th was captured after the Japanese attack on Malaya and 156th served throughout the Near East. The Glasgow Yeomanry were already confirmed in an artillery role by 1939; since 1920 they had been 101st Brigade, Royal Artillery. Converted to 54th and 64th Anti-Tank Regiments, one battery of 54th was captured when Singapore capitulated to the Japanese but the remainder fought in North West Europe

and through the Desert and Italian campaigns. Finally, the Scottish Horse were made into 79th and 80th Medium Regiments; the 79th landing in Europe on the day after D-Day and 80th fighting in Egypt in 1943 before joining 51st (Highland) Division in Italy.

Scotland's only Regular cavalry regiment, The Royal Scots Greys, was still a mounted unit when the war began and, indeed, had fought hard against being mechanised during the late 1920s. Stationed in Palestine, they had been tasked with maintaining a peaceful separation between the two communities of Arabs and Jews. The regiment remained in Palestine until it was mechanised, the last regiment of the Army to be so treated, and left for Egypt in 1942 with its new tanks. Helping to halt the German advance at Alam Halfa in August, they were involved as part of 7th Armoured Division at El Alamein in September. Invasion of Italy and participation in the northward struggle up the peninsula was followed by disembarkation to be re-equipped for the invasion of Europe. The regiment landed in Normandy after D-Day and fought its way from Caen across France into Holland after which, joined with 52nd (Lowland) Division, it invaded Germany and took part in a dash to prevent the Russian Army – advancing from the east – from invading Denmark.

During the dash to Wismar, to form a barrier against the Russians, the Greys carried Canadian infantry on the back of their tanks; men of the 1st Canadian Parachute Battalion. As with the First World War, the Canadian contribution to the war effort was considerable and vast numbers of

174

Pipes and drums of 6th battalion Seaforth Highlanders in Northern Ireland, about 1940.

Canadians served on the continent after D-Day. They had been arriving in Britain since 1939, the 1st Canadian Division landing at Greenock before the end of the year and including among its regiments the 48th Highlanders of Canada as part of the 1st Canadian Infantry Brigade. This Brigade actually formed, briefly, part of the back-up force sent to Cherbourg, along with 52nd (Lowland) Division, in 1940. The Highlanders went to the Brest area of Brittany and, after requisitioning a train to speed their evacuation, left for Britain from St. Malo only a matter of days after they had landed in France. So bad were the communications between a rapidly-crumbling France and Britain that the Toronto Scottish were almost sent to France just at the time that their fellow Scots Canadians were leaving St. Malo.

Gradually the Canadian forces in Britain grew as the siege of the island developed after the fall of France and the Battle of Britain. Still seared into the Canadian consciousness is the raid on Dieppe in 1942 which, despite lengthy planning, was in reality a costly failure even if it provided useful lessons for a repeat performance on a larger scale two years later. Three Canadian Scottish units were involved at Dieppe. The Essex Scottish were to form the left flank of the main attack after the initial assault had been made. The Queen's Own Cameron Highlanders of Canada were to land to the west of Dieppe, join up with tanks and press on inland to take out an aerodrome and establish a defensive perimeter. Three platoons of the Black Watch of Canada were attached to the Royal Regiment of Canada whose task was to land to the east of Dieppe as part of the preliminary

assault, silence a few German batteries and begin constructing the east side of the defensive screen. This latter attack failed completely, with the result that the main assault was laid open to the full force of enfilade fire from entrenched positions and well-sited machine-guns that the Royal Regiment and Black Watch were unable to silence.

The Dieppe raid was a story that illustrates whatever the Scots version of Murphy's Law is: anything that could go wrong, did go wrong. The element of surprise was weakened, timings were put out, support groups failed to materialise or arrived too late to be of any use. One of the few successes was that of 4 Commando which, led by Lord Lovat – emulating the destructive capabilities of his ancestors, succeeded in destroying a strategically-sited battery. 4 Commando's timing and execution was impeccable though and this contributed to its success; the lack of such impeccability elsewhere aided the compound failure of the mission. Although arriving late, and in slightly the wrong place, the Camerons' assault was a qualified success in that they penetrated towards their objective but had to fall back before reaching it because their armoured support had not materialised and because the Germans were clearly in greater strength and better equipped than had been foreseen. They got further inland than any other unit during the raid and suffered severely as a result. The frontal assault of the Essex Scottish ground to a halt as they were scythed down by machine-gunners on their flanks and ahead of them who were supposed to be dealt with by supporting tanks. The tanks were late in arriving and were pinned down

175

HRH The Princess Mary, Princess Royal, inspecting a section of Auxiliary Territorial Service women soldiers attached to 407 (Searchlight) Battery, 4/5 battalion The Royal Scots, Dalkeith Palace 1940. The Princess was Colonel-in-Chief of The Royal Scots.

or picked off as they did arrive by massive concentrations of fire. After the eventual, and equally bloody, evacuation, 500 Essex Scottish were left in Dieppe; most were dead. Of the 52 who returned, 28 were wounded.

In all, sixteen Canadian Scottish battalions served in Europe during the war; three, the 2nd Black Watch of Canada, the Lanark and Renfrew Scottish and the Scots Fusiliers of Canada remained at home in a defensive role. Of the sixteen, four took part in operations in Sicily and Italy: the Perth Regiment, the Cape Breton Highlanders, the 48th Highlanders of Canada and the Seaforth Highlanders of Canada. Each moved to northern Europe during 1945. Five of the sixteen were present among the Canadian forces on D-Day: 1st Black Watch of Canada, the Highland Light Infantry of Canada, the Stormont, Dundas and Glengarry Highlanders, the Cameron Highlanders of Ottawa and the Canadian Scottish. Most of the remaining battalions served in Normandy and north-west Europe during 1944 and 1945. Two Victoria Crosses were won, by Major Frederick Tilston of the Essex Scottish and Private Ernest Smith of the Seaforth Highlanders of Canada.

The fortunes of the three nominally Scottish Division in the years between Dunkirk and D-Day were very different.

The 15th (Scottish) Division formed part of the forces in Britain the entire time and, although reduced in size temporarily in the autumn of 1941, contained nine Scottish Territorial Infantry battalions within its three infantry brigades. During its time of depressed status, which lasted over a year, it continued training and secured the right for all component parts of the Division, irrespective of actual nationality, to wear the Tam o'Shanter bonnet; thus converting all non-Scots to the outward appearance of Scots. Such was an example of the spirit that Divisional loyalty could inspire, particularly when it could identify a common cause. As with most home-based Divisions, the diminishing threat of invasion and the gradual accumulation of successes in North Africa led to a change in training away from a defensive role to that of the aggressor as the tide of the war began to change. By June 1944 it was fully up to strength as part of 8 Army Corps and landed in Normandy a week after D-Day. By that time its 44th Lowland Infantry Brigade comprised 8th Royal Scots, 6th Royal Scots Fusiliers and 6th King's Own Scottish Borderers, all of which battalions had been part of the Division since its formation. Also landing in Normandy as the 46th Highland Infantry Brigade of the Division were 9th Cameronians, 2nd Glasgow Highlanders and 7th Seaforth Highlanders. The Glasgow Highlanders, as we have seen, had been the only kilted battalion of the Highland Light Infantry and the 9th Cameronians were a young battalion of their conspicuously Lowland regiment. Finally, the 227th Highland Infantry Brigade of the Division was formed in 1944 of 10th Highland Light Infantry, 2nd Gordon Highlanders and 2nd Argyll and Sutherland Highlanders, of which only the 10th HLI had

176

France before Dunkirk. Seaforth Highlanders inspect a German anti-tank gun they captured at Boencourt.

France before Dunkirk. Stretcher bearers of the 52nd (Lowland) Division at Conges on the Seine Front. 1940.

177

178

Scottish troops awaiting evacuation from the quayside at St. Malo.

served in the Division previously.

After the 52nd (Lowland) Division had got their breath back from hurrying across the Channel in 1940 they were deployed around London and the Home Counties as part of the reserve in case of invasion. Gradual re-equipment followed, since the Division had been able to bring little larger than their rifles out of France, and in November 1940 it returned to Scotland to provide part of the Scottish anti-invasion forces. As 1942 progressed, and the threat of invasion gradually diminished, so – as with the 15th Division – the training of the 52nd began gradually to reflect a move from a defensive to an aggressive stance. In the case of 52nd though, special training was in order and, after September 1942, an additional scroll appeared on the soldiers' shoulders, below the St. Andrew's shield that was their Divisional formation sign. It contained the word 'Mountain'. Remaining in Scotland and utilising the rugged contours of its upland areas, the Division spent over a year training for mountain warfare in the intention of providing a diversionary thrust against German forces in Norway once the Second Front in Europe was opened. Or so the Germans were led to believe by every tactic that those in charge of the real invasion plans could invent. In the end it never happened and, by the time of D-Day, in June 1944, the Division was already training in Combined Operations based in Inverary on the west coast. After Combined Operations training had occupied six weeks, the Divisional role was changed to that of an Air-Portable Division – paratroops effectively. After training in climbing

mountains, amphibious warfare and jumping out of aeroplanes, the 52nd eventually went to the Low Countries as ordinary conventional infantry in the autumn of 1944. If their training had taught them anything, it was versatility. When it landed on the continent of Europe at the end of 1944 its three infantry brigades were composed the same as they had been in 1939. The 155th contained 7/9th Royal Scots and 4th and 5th King's Own Scottish Borderers; the 156th was made up on 4/5th Royal Scots and 6th and 7th Cameronians and the 157th had 5th and 6th Highland Light Infantry and 1st Glasgow Highlanders, along with 7th Manchester Regiment as an English afterthought.

It is probably fair to say that, of all the Scottish formations involved in the Second World War, the 51st (Highland) Division is the best known. Those to whom the story of the surrender at St. Valéry-en-Caux will come as a surprise will not be able to open any account of the war without encountering one mention of the 51st, or seeing at least one photograph of grinning Jocks in khaki drill erecting yet another example of their formation sign along their route through the Western Desert, Sicily, and finally, NorthWest Europe. The 51st seem to have been truly ubiquitous and their capacity for advertising their presence by the use of their Divisional sign, the conjoined letters HD within a circle, earned them the nickname The Highway Decorators from other Divisions with less high a profile. When they went into the attack at El Alamein at the end of 1942 it was their first battle as a resurrected Division and they did it with a style that was reminiscent of battles long

179

Singapore before the Fall, 1941. Argyll and Sutherland Highlanders exercising
with armoured cars.

ago: led by their pipers. Their advance had been carefully plotted along routes assigned to battalions of the 153rd and 154th Brigades and their objectives identified within those routes by the names of towns associated with each battalion. Thus, on the far right of the Divisional advance, the 5th Black Watch and 1st Gordons faced objectives condenamed Montrose, Abroath and Forfar (all on the edges of Black Watch territory) and, beyond those, Kintore, Braemar, Dufftown and Aberdeen (all well within Gordon country). In the centre, 1st Black Watch advanced towards Perth via Leven, Dollar, Comrie, Killin and Crieff and on the far left the 5th Cameron Highlanders and 7th Black Watch moved via inverness through Dundee to Kirkcaldy. The action of the battalions and brigades of the Division at El Alamein made its reputation, a reputation that remained high – and unthreatened by the presence of any other Scottish Division – until the end of the war. By that time, the 51st had fought throughout the North African campaign and participated in the invasion and capture of Sicily before being ordered to return to Scotland at the end of November 1943 to retrain for the invasion of Europe.

As with the operations during the First World War, those conducted relatively near home during the Second World War received the greatest publicity; the nearer the conflict, the greater the news coverage. While all thus far related was going on in Europe and North Africa, there was another conflict brewing in the Far East and, in December 1941, it boiled over with the Japanese attack on the British forces there. Those British forces included a number of Scottish

battalions spread across the area from India via Singapore to Hong Kong. The 2nd Gordons formed part of 2nd Malaya Infantry Brigade in Singapore; the 2nd Argyll and Sutherland Highlanders were among others in the 12th Indian Infantry Brigade and were stationed on the west coast of Malaya. Both battalions fought in the rearguard action against the Japanese and both were among the forces which surrendered at Singapore in 1942. Both, too, lost nearly as many of their men during Japanese captivity as were killed during the brief Malayan campaign. The 2nd Royal Scots suffered a similar fate in Hong Kong and one that was particularly serious for the regiment as a whole since its 1st battalion had been all but destroyed before Dunkirk.

As with Dunkirk, however, the early reversals in the Far East were not taken advantage of and when British forces re-grouped in India to retake the relinquished territories they included Scottish battalions. 1st Cameronians left India for Rangoon early in 1942 and were in action as part of 1st Burma Brigade within 17th Indian Division before the withdrawal into India later in the year; their casualties were considerable and the battalion reduced to less than a company by the time of the retreat. The revived battalion returned to Burma as part of the 111th Brigade during the Chindit campaign. A re-formed 1st Royal Scots were part of the 6th British Infantry Brigade of 26th Indian Infantry Division during the Arakan campaign of 1943 and fought throughout the campaign for the recapture of Burma, including the battle of Kohima and the advance on Mandalay. 2nd King's

180

The Gordon Highlanders in Singapore were engaged in constructing anti-invasion obstacles. Here officers are listening to a talk on anti-tank methods, 1941.

Own Scottish Borderers joined 59th Indian Infantry Brigade of 7th Indian division in 1943 and fought too in the Arakan, at Imphal and during the advance on Rangoon. 1st Royal Scots Fusiliers, after being part of an expedition (which also included their 2nd battalion and that of the Cameronians) to capture Madagascar in 1942, joined 29th Infantry Brigade of 36th Indian Infantry Division for the Burma campaign.

Other Scots and Scottish battalions served in the re-establishment of a British presence in the Far East until the end of the war in 1945. Theirs was a forgotten war, a war fought under dreadful climatic conditions and requiring considerable fortitude in the face of hardships which little of their training accustomed them to. Not since the 1890s had British troops soldiered aggressively in the Burmese jungles and then, as for other wars in Burma during the nineteenth century, their enemies had been little match for superior Western technology. Against the rapidly-moving, and frequently-suicidal, Japanese considerable tactical rethinking was necessary and a war fought which summoned every reserve of gallantry and patience.

As with the First World War, there are numerous campaign and regimental histories which cover in exhaustive detail each and every action of the Scottish battalions which participated in the Second World War. Because the war is still very much within living memory, although its commemoration for public entertainment by the moving picture industry has slackened in favour of more recent cataclysms, it still has great power as a historical subject. However, it was a propaganda war, by each of the combatants with varying degrees of success. It was a war of ideologies, of cultural and racial genocide, a war that brought the civilian into the front line. Glasgow had its Blitz as did London and Scotland's population now is richer as a result of the immigration from central Europe that the war necessitated. The will to win the Second World War was recognised early on as being as important as possessing the materiel and equipment and this is where the use of the media by government became especially relevant. Although the inter-war years and the war itself had resulted in a greater degree of sophistication further down the social scale, it is of relevance to note how the archetypal figure of the Scottish Highland piper appeared regularly at Victory parades in North African villages, Sicilian towns, Italian cities (and all their equivalents in northern Europe) whenever good newsreel coverage of the fighting soldiers was required. Although dressed in khaki Battledress blouse above his kilt and with boots and short puttees rather than hose and spats, the personification of Scotland in the figure of the piper did much to inspire audiences at home for whom the realities of the war manifested themselves in rationing and air-raids. From being a figure first despised and feared through one to be laughed at and suborned, this kilted representative of Scotland played as much of a part in the modern propaganda war which kept people going at

181

A section of Seaforth Highlanders, Western Desert, 1943. The soldiers retain hose-tops and gaiter flashes and the officer sports a *sgian dubh* in his right hose-top.

Major David Stirling of the Scots Guards with some of the Long Range Desert Group.

182

183

Scots Guards prepare to receive a German attack.

184

Scots Guards accompany Matilda tanks in an advance.

185A

Men of the 2nd battalion Scots Guards in the Western Desert.

185B

A Scots Guardsman cools his feet in the Mediterranean after a march in the desert.

186

Pipes and drums of 2nd battalion The Royal Scots on the flight deck of an escort aircraft carrier, Gibraltar 1943.

187

Men of The Black Watch view a German anti-aircraft half-track knocked out in the Sicily campaign.

188

Men of 1st battalion Scots Guards boarding the *Derbyshire*
from which they will take part in the Anzio operation. Naples harbour,
1944.

189A

Scots Guards searching for snipers among the ruins of Monte Cassino.
Castle Hill can be seen in the middle distance.

Scots Guards on a mopping-up patrol through Monte Cassino.

Pipes and drums of 1st battalion London Scottish at Pola, Italy 1945.

191

• A patrol led by Captain Ogilvie of the Glider Pilot Regiment, who landed in his kilt, about to set out for Arnhem after clearing the landing zone, 1944.

192

Men of the 51st Highland Division being carried into a position to cut off Germans escaping from s'Hertogenbosch 1944.

193

Infantry of 2nd battalion Argyll and Sutherland Highlanders advancing on Churchill tanks of 3rd battalion Scots Guards, 1944.

194

2nd battalion Gordon Highlanders approach Tilburg, 1944.

195

Pipe band of 10th Highland Light Infantry, 15th Scottish
Division, march past Major-General Barber DSO. Mulmeese, 1944.

195B

Patrols of 5/7 Gordon Highlanders house-clearing at Kaatscheuvel, 1944.

Men of 4/5 battalion Royal Scots Fusiliers, 1945.

196

197

Private T. Getty of Dundee. 1945.

Lieutenant-Colonel Pearson, 8th Royal Scots, with Lieutenant-Colonel de Winton
DSO, 2nd Gordon Highlanders, consult the map on the road to Kleve, 1945.

198

199

Sniper of 5th battalion Black Watch waits and watches
for unwary Germans, Gennep, 1945.

200

2nd battalion Gordon Highlanders with captured Nazi
flag. 1945.

201

Queen's Own Cameron Highlanders march through Kure, Japan,
when the flags of the Commonwealth nations were unfurled
ceremoniously over Japanese soil for the first time, 1946.

home as he did, *en masse*, in emulating his ancestors by leading his fellow soldiers into battle. The perennial fascination exercised by the Scottish soldier was made much of during the Second World War and since each regiment, Highland or Lowland, seemed able to produce a kilted piper at the drop of a Tam o'Shanter, it was natural that Divisions such as the 51st should derive such personal propaganda advantage from the nation that they represented. Historians could tell them that it had ever been thus and that non-Scottish regiments stood no chance in the face of such flagrant advertising. The realities of the Second World War, as the effective end of what little global supremacy Britain possessed, took several years to penetrate after 1945. For several decades after the Victory celebrations a nation that was about to begin giving away an Empire and searching for a role would continue to require the services and qualities peculiar to Scotland's soldiers.

Pipe-Major John Maclellan, Seaforth Highlanders, 1946.

CHAPTER TEN

KEEPING THE PEACE

1945 to 2000

At the end of the war with Japan in August 1945, the British Army, men as well as women, consisted of almost three million people. Like their predecessors in 1918, their first priority was to get out of uniform and back to civilian life as quickly as possible. Although gradual demobilisation whittled the Army to a more manageable size, remaining commitments worldwide necessitated the retention of substantial bodies of soldiers across the globe. Most of these were conscripts who had been called up during the war and who had to serve out their time policing the last days of the old Empire before being allowed to go home. The nature of the soldier during the war had been that of the conscript; the civilian in arms. For eighteen years after the war, Britain's involvements all over the world required that a substantial part of her Army would continue to be formed of conscripted young men.

In 1947 the National Service Act was passed in order, effectively, to maintain the *status quo* and to keep the Army up to a reduced strength in order to cope with international commitments. The original implementation of the Act involved one year's service, followed by six in the Reserve, by each British male over the age of 18 without previous military service. It was felt that the Army of 305,000 men which would result from this would be adequate. Events building up in the Far East rapidly necessitated the lengthening of the period of National Service, first to eighteen months in 1948 and then to two years in 1950. This latter extension of the period resulted in an Army of 442,000. Although its size gradually reduced during the 1950s, this was the Army which fought in Korea, which was humiliated at Suez and which helped give away the Empire. It was not a wholly conscript Army, but in 1957 – when Harold Macmillan recognised that the end of both Empire and National Service was nigh, of an Army strength of 373,000 over half were National Servicemen. National Service necessarily trawled the population with a net of very small mesh and few escaped, although many wished to do so at the time. The result for the Army was really a continuation of its war-time composition of all walks of life, all social groups and all standards of mental and physical attitude. The strength of the National Service Army was that it possessed great talent and produced many excellent non-commission officers. The weakness was that although when

its conscripts were good they were very, very good, when they were bad they were awful, and far below the standard acceptable in a Regular recruit. In addition to this unavoidable problem, there was also the fact that only by the end of the conscript's two-year stint was he beginning to shape up at all as a soldier, by which time he was about to leave and be of no further use to the Army which had just, therefore, wasted two years training him. There is also evidence to support the suggestion that the National Serviceman cost the Army more in terms of keep, training and accommodation than did the Regular. All in all it was a rather bad bargain and one which the Army of the 1980s is not anxious to repeat. Had successive British administrations after the war realised, or been able to admit to themselves, that the Empire had had its day, it is likely that National Service would have been ended much sooner. The fact that it was finally abolished in 1960 (the last National Serviceman was demobilised in 1963), may have been a significant contributory factor to the massive changes in British society during the 1960s.

Britain had divested herself of two increasingly troublesome parts of Empire during the late 1940s, one an old member of the Imperial Firm, the other newer and less traditionally-entrenched: India and Palestine. Indian movements for independent status had continued throughout the war and increased in number and volume after 1945. Independence had been seen as inevitable since the 1930s; it was more a question of 'when' rather than 'if'. The 1st battalion Royal Scots Fusiliers were one of the last British battalions to leave India. After spending two years on internal security duties in the subcontinent, their last few weeks, as India disintegrated around them, were harrowing.

Palestine had been becoming a steadily more unhealthy place for British soldiers too since the end of the war, as large-scale Jewish immigration began and the Arab population reacted against it. British troops were caught between the two communities but, unlike the policing role that had been necessary in the years immediately before the war (when British troops were essentially protecting Jewish settlers from being massacred by Arabs), the situation between 1945 and 1948 was rather different. Now, the British were seen as the enemy by the Jewish immigrants who were bent upon the creation of Israel and did not want

203

Presentation of new colours to 1st battalion Highland Light Infantry, Suez, 1948.

the immigration process slowed. Many of the members of the two most prominent Jewish terrorist gangs, the Haganah and the Irgun, had been trained in the British Army during the war and inflicted numerous casualties upon their former comrades-in-arms in the name of Israel. It was an impossible situation for Britain and one which had been wished upon her at the end of the First World War. When British forces left Palestine in 1948 they could not have realised that the campaign which they were leaving behind would be the first of many similar actions during the post-war decades: ones necessitating the fighting of native terrorism by a combination of police and army tactics. Some of the British soldiers who served during the Palestine campaign gained valuable experience in Near Eastern terrorism and many of 1st Argyll and Sutherland High-landers were to take that experience with them to Aden a decade and a half later.

Long before such experience was necessary for the Argylls however, a conventional war loomed in Korea and the regiment (its two battalions having been amalgamated a couple of months after the 1st battalion returned from Palestine) moved from Hong Kong to Korea in August 1950. The 1st Argylls (the battalion number was retained in the studiously-observed belief that the 2nd battalion was not dead but merely sleeping heavily) were the first Scottish battalion to serve in Korea as part of the 27th Brigade within the 1st Commonwealth Division. The Division's composition was all that its title implied. It contained units

from India, Canada, Australia and New Zealand as well as ones from the United Kingdom. In all, four Scottish infantry battalions were to serve in Korea and the Black Watch of Canada's 2nd battalion went out to join the 25th Brigade in October 1953, when the war was virtuall over. There was little overlap in the service of Scots battalions in Korea and one tended to replace another after a tour of duty of varying length. The 1st Argylls remained until April 1951 when 1st King's Own Scottish Borderers arrived, who remained until August 1952. 1st Black Watch moved to Korea in June 1952 but as part of 29th Brigade, whereas 1st King's Own Scottish Borderers remained in 27th and 28th Brigades. The Black Watch left in July 1953 as 1st Royal Scots arrived but by that time the war was effectively over and, although the Royal Scots were credited with the exuberant expenditure of a little machine-gun fire, they did no actual fighting.

Such was far from the case in the experience of the first three Scottish battalions to serve in the Korean War. A measure of their involvement in the savage, often hand-to-hand, and frequent last-ditch fighting which characterised the nature of war at the sharp end in Korea was that, of four Victoria Crosses awarded for the war, two were given to men of Scottish regiments. Such a yardstick is of course superficial and inadequate and takes no account of the daily unrecognised acts of gallantry which occur in any and every war. However, in the absence of any rule of thumb other than the equally-unsatisfactory one of casualty figures, it must suffice. This is particularly so when one realises that

204

Pipe-Major Donald Maclean and Drum-Major James Watson. King's Guard Pipe Band at Balmoral Castle, 1947.

205

1st battalion Gordon Highlanders taking part in The King's Birthday Parade, Berlin, 1950.

the other two VCs were awarded for the Battle of the Imjin River to two officers of The Gloucestershire Regiment. In September 1950 Major Kenneth Muir, second-in-command of the 1st Argyll and Sutherland Highlanders, won his VC posthumously (and also a posthumous American Distinguished Service Cross) for his tenacious gallantry in holding a virtually idenfensible position while at the same time overseeing the removal of wounded soldiers. Over a year later Scotland's other Korea VC was awarded to Private William Speakman of 1st King's Own Scottish Borderers who persistently drove off bodies of Chinese troops by repeated grenade charges. Bill Speakman was an Englishman, serving in the Black Watch but attached to The King's Own Scottish Borderers. His VC and medals are now preserved in Edinburgh Castle. During the same action as that in which Speakman won his VC, a National Service subaltern of his regiment, William Purves, gained a Distinguished Service Order, a decoration normally awarded to more senior commanders of men. Speakman's original regiment, The Black Watch, distinguished themselves at the First and Third Battles of the Hook in November 1952 and May 1953; eight officers and men were decorated for gallantry after the first battle.

Of the 20,000 British servicemen who fought in Korea, it is estimated that 2,000 were conscripts, a proportion kept deliberately low by excluding from active service anyone over the age of nineteen. Despite this move, which was a sensible piece of bad-publicity avoidance by government, it is also estimated that by the end of the conflict some bat-

talions, including 1st King's Own Scottish Borderers, may have had up to 60% National Servicemen, officers and other ranks, in them. Korea was a bloody war, few wars are not, and the drain on manpower may have necessitated the use of theoretically disqualified National Servicemen.

More emotive than Korea, from the point of view of the involvement of National Servicemen, was the use of British troops in Malaya. Of the two dozen or so British infantry battalions which served in Malaya during the Emergency from 1948 to 1960, six were Scottish and, since National Service was in full swing during the whole time, a substantial proportion of those who served in the steamy jungles against the Chinese terrorists were conscripts. The very personal nature of jungle warfare of the type required in Malaya led to battalions competing with each other for the highest number of terrorists liquidated; 1st Cameronians are recorded as having cut 125 notches on the battalion's belt, 1st King's Own Scottish Borderers managed eight. Jungle warfare is frequently even more savagely unpleasant than war in the open and, when it is mixed with that lethal combination of politics and national determination, of ideology and independence, it generates gross inhumanity. Few prisoners were taken in Malaya, other than those required for intelligence purposes, and the prospects for wounded British soldiers or those captured alive were not good. In an episode that they would probably prefer to forget, a 2nd Scots Guard patrol, chiefly of National Servicemen, murdered twenty-six Malay villagers on suspicion of being or aiding terrorists. Such incidents were neither uncommon

206

A platoon of The Black Watch leaving on patrol, Korea 1953.

nor restricted to Scottish regiments and even their brutality pales beside that demonstrated in later Far Eastern conflicts.

Malaya was essentially a police action, aimed at stabilising the country in the slow progress towards independence. Operations in Kenya against the Mau-Mau between 1952 and 1956 and in Cyprus between 1955 and 1959 were little different in their essential political aim and use of soldiers. Among many others, 1st Black Watch served in Kenya and 1st Royal Scots Fusiliers and 1st Gordon Highlanders in Cyprus.

The real indication of the state of the dental equipment of the British lion was demonstrated at Suez in 1956 when, after a bungled assault owing a lot to political indecision at the highest level, the joint British and French forces trying to do a Garnet Wolseley on Colonel Nasser were told to stop it by the United Nations. Realising that perhaps they should not have done it anyway (or done it properly at the very least) the Allies did as they were told and withdrew. Only the 1st Royal Scots represented Scottish interests at this particular demonstration of the way things had changed since the days of Palmerstonian gunboat diplomacy.

By the end of the 1950s the world was conspicuously and rapidly changing. Space-age technology had arrived, the Cold War intensified, the Union Flag was being hauled down from flagpoles around the world and people coming more and more to question the hitherto largely-unquestioned decisions, made from them by their elected representatives. With reduced overseas commitments

Britain no longer needed a large army and the ending of National Service in 1960 occurred deliberately in the middle of widespread cuts in the Army as a whole. Regiments which had been reduced to single battalions after the war were now given the alternatives of amalgamation or disbandment. Most chose amalgamation on the basis that marriage is pre-ferable to death, even if the union is an enforced one of incompatible types.

In Scotland the Royal Scots Fusiliers and Highland Light Infantry amalgamated in 1959 to form the Royal Highland Fusiliers and the Seaforth Highlanders and Cameron High-landers merged in 1961 to form the Queen's Own high-landers (Seaforth and Camerons). Elements of both partners were retained in the new regiments but the late 50s saw the beginnings of an idea that has yet to have its death certificate signed. As will have been apparent in this tale, the story of the British Army is really one of many stories of many regiments, generally acting together but always separately. For some, the regimental system is one of the greatest strengths of the British Army. It inspires group loyalty in a way that its antithesis, a Corps of Infantry and one of Cavalry – containing just numbered units instead of old names and traditions, would not have the power to do. The creation in 1959 of Infantry Brigades was a first step towards the concept of a Corps of Infantry and its outward sign was that within a Brigade only one cap-badge would be worn, although regimental collar-badges, facing colours, tartans and buttons would remain unaffected. What it took away with one hand it gave back with another in a way that

207

Observation post manned by The Black Watch, Korea 1952.

Soldiers of The Black Watch use a Browning 0.30 inch calibre machine-gun against Chinese positions, Korea 1952.

208

209 A

209 B

A mortar observer watches for targets across a valley in Korea. The men belong to 1st battalion, Kings Own Scottish Borderers.

Private William Speakman V.C. $\longrightarrow$

210

Victoria Cross 1951 and medals won by Private William Speakman, King's Own Scottish Borderers.

211

Korea, 1952. Two soldiers take a smoke break. They are wearing
protective vests against shell fragments.

all attempts at making the British Army uniform had done
since the first attempts at standardisation in the middle of
the eighteenth century. In Scotland, the Lowland Brigade
contained the Lowland regiments and the Highland Brigade
the Highland ones. This (frankly rather silly) compromise
persisted for a decade until the formation of The Scottish
Division, which grouped all the Scottish regiments together
under one central administration for recruiting and all other
purposes, except purely regimental ones, and restored the
regimental bonnet badges. During the process further
reductions of the Army had been attempted and led to con-
sidrable apprehension in Scotland where, for a variety of
reasons, the bulk of the civilian population had gradually
grown to become close to its soldiers and to take a rather
proprietorial attitude to them. In 1968 the Cameronians
chose disbandment as an alternative to amalgamation and
so slipped quietly away just twenty years short of their three
hundredth birthday. Rather more noise was made when the
Argyll and Sutherland Highlanders were threatened with
similar treatment and so they were merely reduced to
company strength for a couple of years until the need for
soldiers to confront renewed problems in Northern Ireland
resulted in their growth back to full battalion complement.
The 2nd Scots Guards suffered a similar fate for a brief
period at the same time.

The end-of-Empire operations persisted through most of
the 1960s and involved Scottish soldiers in places as diverse

as Brunei and Aden. It was, perhaps, slightly ironic (but not
untypical if one recollects the degree of gratitude usually
showered upon soldiers by successive governments) that the
two regiments for whom the anti-terrorist campaign in Aden
between 1964 and 1967 had resulted in such high media
profiles should be the ones that government proposed to
disband, with tactless timing, once the campaign in South
Arabia was over. It was purely by accident that the
Cameronians and Argylls were the junior Lowland and
Highland regiments respectively and had acquitted
themselves efficiently in Aden.

Throughout all this, after 1945, as this book is being
written and for the foreseeable future, Britain maintained,
maintains and will continue to maintain a presence in
Germany, chiefly under the title of British Army of the
Rhine (BAOR). The Army in Germany had been converted
in the late 1940s from one with a mere occupying role to one
with a defensive capability as the Cold War intensified.
Under the post-war Labour government BAOR grew from
two passive Divisions to five potentially-aggressive ones. In
the early 1950s it numbered 80,000 men and by the end of
the decade it had shrunk to 55,000, a size that remained
fairly constant for twenty years. Infantry battalions could,
and can, expect to undertake tours of duty of two or three
years in Germany, either in BAOR or in Berlin, but their
comrades in the artillery or in the armoured regiments can
expect much longer service, frequently more than ten years

212

Comet cruiser tanks in service with The Lothians and Border Horse, 1951.

213

Sentries at Edinburgh Castle, Scots Guards, 1951.

Proposed No 1 Dress, Lowland regiments, 1950.

216

Scots Guards rehearse marching off their Colours, 1951.

at a time. As Scotland's only armoured regiment, The Royal Scots Greys have served back and forth in Germany or at home since the 1960s, with the occasional operational tour in the Middle East and peace-keeping duties in armoured cars or light tanks in Cyprus and Northern Ireland. As part of the Defence Cuts at the end of the 1960s they too were amalgamated, with 3rd Carabiniers, to form The Royal Scots Dragoon Guards (Caribiniers and Greys) in 1971.

The picturesque qualities of the public face of the Scottish regiments make them generally popular in Germany but the nature of their occupation is such that, like most British troops, they have little to do with the civilian population. Parallels that are drawn between the British soldier in Germany and his Imperial predecessor in India are too simplistic but the fact remains that Germany is not, and rarely has been, a popular posting for the soldier. To all intents and purposes he might as well be in Britain when in camp, yet – because of his general lack of linguistic ability – he is necessarily confined to his camp and its entertainments, which are both limited in scope and governed by regulations which do not apply in the outside world. In that outside world in Germany however, unless he is a member of the military band or Pipes and Drums, he is likely to find life difficult. The rearming of Germany and the creation of the *Bundeswehr* in the 1950s (in the face of French outrage – with much ostentatious Gallic touching of sword-hilts and surreptitious packing of valises) naturally reduced the burden which the defence of Germany in the face of the

supposed threat from the East imposed upon Britain but it is doubtful if representations from NATO will allow a complete British withdrawal from the continent. Some Scottish regiments have been more popular than others in Germany and with the German civilian population. Like many people outside the Army, few German civilians are aware of regimental differences between the Scottish regiments and so bad behaviour by one tartaned battalion will inevitably lead to prejudice against all. Few battalions have gone as far, fortunately, as 1st Cameronians did in 1962 when considerable damage was done to a bar in Minden and the aggressive qualities combined with the diminutive stature of many of the men of the battalion resulted, after intense media publicity, in the revelation that the battalion was known to the German civilians as *Giftzwerge* – poison dwarves. Brawling and aggression are not, and were not, confined either to the Cameronians or to the Scottish regiments and incidents such as that in Minden in 1962 were, and are unfortunately, not uncommon. They were a result of the isolation experienced by the British soldier in Germany and the growth of younger generations there who resent and misunderstand the presence and function of the British Army.

Equally difficult has been the role of the British soldier in Northern Ireland. That unhappy and divided province flared into open and bloody discord in 1969 and, ever since – but now in gradually diminishing numbers, British soldiers have had to be stationed there as the instruments of govern-

217

Edinburgh Military Tattoo 1952.

ment policy. The Northern Ireland experience, although not dissimilar from police-and-military actions fought overseas since the end of the war, is sufficiently different that techniques and modifications of street-fighting strategy have been necessitated in order that the Army may remain on top of the situation. Every Scottish infantry battalion has done tours of duty in Northern Ireland, tours which have revealed the strengths now inherent in the post-National Service Army. It is of interest to note, for instance, that very, very few of the battalion commanders who have served in the province have done other than fully competent, and in some cases brilliant, jobs. Such is the nature of the Army officer of the 1980s; more professional than ever, more sophisticated, wider-read, better-travelled and better-educated. Urban peace-keeping duties require the expertise of a particular type of soldier and it is of interest to note that the Scottish soldier who comes from an urban background in an industrial town such as Glasgow, or even Aberdeen or Dundee, is better able to cope with the situation on the streets in Belfast or Derry than his rural comrade who has to have instilled the sort of streetwise experience which tend to be inherent in the urban male of the modern era. On rural exercise, of course, the reverse is likely to be the case.

The Army now takes Germany and Northern Ireland for granted. So does most of the civilian population. Until 1982 the same attitude would have applied to a cluster of sheep-covered rocks off the coast of Argentina and, even if the majority of people had been able to locate the Falkland Islands on a globe, it is unlikely that one in a hundred could

have named a reason for their strategic importance. The latter lack of knowledge may still apply outside certain anonymous buildings in London but no-one can now claim not to have heard of these islands. Although the names of strategic objectives for which so many brave men died so recently are now fading from what passes for the popular memory, it is still possible to awaken a flicker of response by the use of the words Goose Green, or Mount Longdon or, in Scotland especially, Tumbledown Mountain. 2nd battalion Scots Guards were involved throughout the campaign to recapture the Falklands and acquitted themselves expensively but efficiently, in the tradition of their regiment, in the taking of Tumbledown. Since the establishment of a British military presence on the Falklands, Scottish battalions still serve tours of duty there among the penguins. It is unlikely that any near future Defence Cuts will markedly affect a strongpoint won at such cost to political careers and soldiers' lives.

Cuts in expenditure on the Army in the years after the end of the war have affected every aspect of its life. Although the soldier is now better paid, housed, fed and cared for than ever, an overall lack of money for training and equipment makes life very frustrating for people whose chief objective is the pursuit of excellence yet who have to make do with adequacy some of the time and inadequacy frequently. The observation that It Was Ever Thus, at least in time of peace, fails to satisfy the new breed of professional soldier now comprising the Army.

Most swingeing of all cuts have been those on the

218

4/5 battalion Gordon Highlanders (T.A.) Coronation Party No. 1 Dress, 1953.

Territorial Army in the years since 1945, a force which was allowed to run down considerably until it reached the point in 1967 when it had almost ceased effectively to exist. In that year the creation of the Territorial and Army Volunteer Reserve brought it to a small establishment of 50,000 men and women and in Scotland gradually moved the Territorial battalions of the infantry regiments away from them and towards larger groupings based on Highland and Lowland areas. The resulting creation of 51st Highland Volunteers and 52nd Lowland Volunteers rationalised the Scottish Territorials and these units continue, the 51st with three battalions and the 52nd with two. The Scottish Yeomanry has gradually disappeared in the forty years of peace; regiments have been amalgamated and finally disbanded until at the time of writing only the Ayrshire Yeomanry still exist, as a squadron of the Queen's Own Yeomanry.

The change in British society since 1945 has been more rapid than in any previous similar period of history. Since a nation's army naturally reflects, in armed microcosm, the society from which it is drawn, one should naturally assume that the Army has undergone similarly wide-ranging and significant changes. It has and it hasn't. Many things remain the same. The bulk of officers are still drawn, in the infantry and cavalry, from the public-school educated upper middle-class; most of the soldiers still come from the rural or urban poor. More officers than ever have University degrees; less hunt regularly. More soldiers have educational certificates before they enlist; less need to be taught the rudiments of personal hygiene. Non-commissioned officers still run the

army at regimental level, but do it less on lung-power and brutality alone, yet still with the kind of devastating efficiency that leaves one gasping with admiration. There is greater sophistication but there is concomitantly greater dissatisfaction. The role of women in the Army is greater than ever and becoming less domestic or welfare-oriented: many infantry battalions now draw their Assistant Adjutants from the Women's Royal Army Corps. Soldiers are marrying younger and assuming domestic responsibilities quicker than ever; they are also getting in debt and getting divorced quicker too. Fewer officers are making the Army their career but there are still regiments where several generations of the same family have provided officers; in an increasing number of cases these new officers are the sons of warrant officers or non-commissioned officers. As technology advances at an ever-increasing rate, and requiring increased Defence Expenditure, so it follows that the recruit will need, more and more, either to be technically adept on recruitment or be capable of becoming so. A shrinking Army needs less recruits than ever yet, in times of large-scale unemployment, there are many potential soldiers knocking on the doors of Army Careers Offices. This is especially so in Scotland where going for a soldier lacks the social stigma still attached to the profession elsewhere in Britain. The Army can afford to pick and choose and it chooses increasingly selectively, rejecting sometimes forty per cent of applicants at initial interview and more later in the induction process.

As the Scottish fighting man approaches the last thirteen

219

Royal Scots Greys escort the Royal coach, along the Royal Mile, Edinburgh, June 1953.

years of the second millenium of his story he can expect change to accelerate but he can still expect much to remain the same. He will, as a new recruit, be introduced to all the mythology which makes him what he is, which passes for history in his regiment and which has made his regiment what it is. If he is an officer, he will be gradually introduced to the customs of the Mess, as generations of his predecessors have been, but less required to be purely a social ornament. Indeed, if that is his concept of soldiering, the chances of him getting as far as having his accent, clothes and table manners scrutinised are very slim and will be positively emaciated by the end of the century. Scotland will continue to provide a significant proportion of Britain's soldiers; a more than significant proportion per head of her population. The difference in identity between Highlander and Lowlander will continue to blur but that between the man from the West coast and the man from the East persist. Regimental character may be expected to continue yet be perceptible only to the indoctrinated. For the majority, the Scottish soldier will remain unchanged and a figment of a mass imagination which finds mythology easier to comprehend than fact; romance more attractive than reality. Equipped, trained and inured to fight a modern war of unimaginable horror, to keep a thankless peace amidst communities bent on mutual dismemberment or to provide an expendable shield guaranteed to last just long enough for the last politician to escape into the last bunker, the Scottish soldier will do what he has been best at doing since his creation. He will endure.

220

A detachment of Cameronians, Edinburgh Castle, 1953.

221

Pipe-Major Crabbe and drummer of the Scots Guards, Erskine
Camp, Malaya, 1950.

222

Cameronian jungle patrol display captured Communist flags and cap, Malayan Emergency.

223A

General Erskine accepts the salute from men of The Black Watch engaged in operations against the Mau-Mau in Kenya, 1954.

223B

Internal Security Drill being practised by King's Own Scottish Borderers in Aden.

224

Rifle inspection, London Scottish, 1954. Below, members of the regimental band find an alternative use for a bass drum.

225

226

The Black Watch, Edinburgh, 1958.

Highland Light Infantry. Army Exhibition, 1958.

227

228

Presentation of Colours to 1st battalion Queen's Own Cameron Highlanders at Balmoral Castle, 1955.

HM Queen Elizabeth The Queen Mother inspects The Black Watch, Redford Barracks, 1958.

229

230

231

Royal Highland Fusiliers, Old Anniesland Glasgow. Presentation of new Colours by
HRH The Princess Margaret, 1959.

232

Pipes and drums of The Royal Highland Fusiliers lead the guard into Holyrood Palace, 1959.

233

Royal Highland Fusiliers and London Scottish mount guard at Holyrood Palace, 1959.

Scots Guards mortar team in action, 1960.

234

8/9 battalion The Royal Scots (T.A.), Edinburgh, 1962.

235

236

1st battalion, Cameronians, Edinburgh Castle.

237

1st battalion, Cameronians, 1968.

238

Armoured Personnel Carrier, 1969.

239

Amalgamation Parade, Royal Scots Greys, 1971.

240

241

A patrol of the Queen's Own Highlanders search for rebels in the jungle of Brunei.

242

The cutting edge of The Royal Scots Dragoon Guards in the 1980s is the Chieftain Main Battle Tank, an example of which is seen here awaiting overhaul at Chilwell Ordnance Depot.

243

Test firing a MILAN wire-guided anti-tank missile. MILAN is served by a two-man team, has a range of 2,000 metres and can penetrate armour of more than 350mm thickness.

244

The Nuclear, Biological and Chemical protective clothing – known colloquially as 'Noddy suits'.

245

Soldiers of the Black Watch in Guyana.

246

A patrol of The Black Watch move towards a German village while on
exercise with the British Army of the Rhine.

247

Northern Ireland. Men of The Black Watch prepare to leave their base on a
routine patrol.

248

Northern Ireland. Men of a Scottish regiment set off on patrol in a stripped-down Land Rover.

249

Northern Ireland. A Ferret scout car manned by soldiers of The Black Watch together with personnel of the 3rd battalion Ulster Defence Regiment.

250

The Falklands War. Scots Guards at Mount Harriet.

Scots Guards digging in on Goat Ridge while being subjected to Argentine artillery fire.

251

252

Scots Guards, Goat Ridge, 1982.

Men of the Scots Guards after hearing the news of the Argentine surrender.

253

254

Men of the Scots Guards rejoice that the war is over.

A Scots Guardsman escorts Argentine prisoners to the rear.

255

256

Scots Guards welcomed home by their
Colonel, HRH The Duke of Kent.

SUGGESTIONS FOR FURTHER READING

GENERAL

Barnett, Correlli *Britain and her army, 1509–1970* Allen Lane, 1970
Brander, Michael *The Scottish highlanders and their regiments* Seeley, Service, 1971
Brereton, J.M. *A guide to the regiments and corps of the British Army* Bodley Head, 1985
Fortescue, J.W. *History of the British Army* 13 volumes Macmillan, 1899–1930
Holmes, Richard *Firing line* Cape, 1985
Keegan, John *The face of battle* Cape, 1976
Leslie, N.B. *Battle honours of the British and Indian armies* Leo Cooper, 1970
McGuffie, T.H. *Rank and file: the common soldier at peace and war, 1642–1914* Hutchinson, 1964
Maxwell, H. (Ed.) *The Lowland Scots regiments* Maclehose 1918
Myatt, Frederick *The soldier's trade: British military developments, 1660–1914* Blandford, 1974
Smurthwaite, David *The Ordnance Survey complete guide to the battlefields of Britain* Webb & Bower, 1984

CHAPTER ONE

Fischer, T.A. *The Scots in Eastern and Western Prussia*, Schulze, 1903
Fischer, T.A. *The Scots in Germany* Schulze, 1902

CHAPTER TWO

Black, C.S. *Scottish battles* Brown, Son & Ferguson, 1936
Childs, John *The army of Charles II* Routledge & Kegan Paul, 1976
Childs, John *The army, James II, and the glorious revolution* Manchester University Press, 1980
Dalton, C. *The Scots Army 1661–1688: with memoirs of the commanders-in-chief* Eyre & Spottiswoode, 1909
Donaldson, G. *Scotland: James V–James VII* Oliver & Boyd, 1978

CHAPTER THREE

Ferguson, William *Scotland: 1689 to the present* Oliver & Boyd, 1979
Lenman, Bruce *The Jacobite Risings in Britain, 1689–1746* Eyre Methuen, 1980
Lenman, Bruce *The Jacobite clans of the Great Glen, 1650–1784* Methuen, 1984
Prebble, John *Culloden* Secker & Warburg, 1961
Prebble, John *Glencoe: the story of the massacre* Secker & Warburg, 1966
Scouller, R.E. *The armies of Queen Anne* Clarendon Press, 1966
Taylor, William *The military roads in Scotland* David & Charles, 1976
Warner, Philip *British battlefields: Scotland and the border* Osprey, 1975

CHAPTER FOUR

Guy, Alan J. *Oeconomy and discipline: officership and administration in the British Army, 1714–63* Manchester University Press, 1985
Hughes, B.P. *Open fire: artillery tactics from Marlborough to Wellington* Antony Bird, 1983
Katcher, Philip *King George's army, 1775–1783: a handbook of British, American and German regiments* Osprey, 1973
Prebble, John *The Highland Clearances* Secker & Warburg, 1963
Prebble, John *Mutiny* Secker & Warburg, 1975

CHAPTER FIVE

Brett-James, Antony *Life in Wellington's army* Allen & Unwin, 1972
Strachan, Hew *From Waterloo to Balaclava: tactics, technology and the British Army, 1815–1854* Cambridge University Press, 1985
Strachan, Hew *Wellington's legacy: the reform of the British Army, 1830–1854* Manchester University Press, 1984
Sutherland, John *Men of Waterloo* F. Muller, 1967

CHAPTER SIX

Baker, Harold *The territorial force: a manual of its law and administration* J. Murray, 1909
Cunningham, Hugh *The volunteer force: a social and political history 1859–1908* Croom Helm, 1975
Goodspeed, D.J. *Battle royal: a history of the Royal Regiment of Canada, 1862–1962* Royal Regiment of Canada Association, Toronto, 1962
Jenkins, Gwyn Harries *The army in Victorian society* Routledge & Kegan Paul, 1977
Pakenham, Thomas *The Boer War* Weidenfeld & Nicolson, 1979
Skelley, Alan Ramsay *The Victorian army at home* Croom Helm, 1977
Spiers, Edward M. *The army and society 1815–1914* Longman, 1980

CHAPTER SEVEN

Allinson, Sydney *The Bantams: the untold story of World War I* Howard Baker, 1981
Ascoli, David *The Mons Star: the British Expeditionary Force, 1914* Harrap, 1981
Beckett, Ian F.W. and Simpson, Keith *A nation in arms: a social study of the British Army in the First World War* Manchester University Press, 1985
Gill, Douglas and Dallas, Gloden *The unknown army: mutinies in the British Army in World War I* Verso, 1985
Hay, Ian *Their name liveth: the book of the Scottish National War Memorial* SNWM, 1985
Liddle, Peter H. (Ed.) *Home fires and foreign fields: British social and military experience in the First World War* Brassey, 1985
McLaren, Eva Shaw *A history of the Scottish Women's Hospitals* Hodder & Stoughton, 1919

CHAPTER EIGHT

Higham, Robin *Armed forces in peacetime: Britain 1918–1940, a case study* Foulis, 1962
Jeffrey, Keith *The British Army and the crisis of empire, 1918–22* Manchester University Press, 1984
Luvaas, Jay *The education of an army: British military thought, 1815–1940* Cassell, 1965

CHAPTER NINE

Beattie, Kim *Dileas: history of the 48th Highlanders of Canada* 48th Highlanders of Canada, Toronto, 1957
Fraser, David *And we shall shock them: the British Army in the Second World War* Hodder & Stoughton, 1983
Saunders, Hilary St. George *The green beret: the story of the Commandos, 1940–1945* Michael Joseph, 1949
Woollcombe, Robert *Lion rampant* Chatto & Windus, 1955

CHAPTER TEN

Dewar, Michael *The British Army in Northern Ireland* Arms & Armour Press, 1985
Dewar, Michael *Brush fire wars: minor campaigns of the British Army since 1945* R. Hale, 1984

Gander, Terry *Encyclopedia of the modern British Army* Patrick Stephens, 1982
Hamill, Desmond *Pig in the middle: the army in Northern Ireland, 1969–1984* Methuen, 1985
Parker, Tony *Soldier, soldier* Heinemann, 1985
Royle, Trevor *The best years of their lives: the national service experience, 1945–63* Michael Joseph, 1986
Stanhope, Henry *The soldiers: an anatomy of the British Army* Hamish Hamilton, 1979

MEDALS

Abbott, P.E. and Tamplin, J.M.A. *British gallantry awards* Nimrod Dix, 1981
Crook, M.J. *The evolution of the Victoria Cross* Midas, 1975
Gordon, L.L. *British battles and medals* Spink, 1979
Purves, Alec A. *The medals, decorations and orders of the Great War* Hayward, 1975
Smyth, Sir John *The story of the Victoria Cross* Muller, 1963

UNIFORMS AND EQUIPMENT

Carman, W.Y. *British military uniforms from contemporary pictures: Henry VII to the present day* Leonard Hill, 1957
Chappell, Mike *British cavalry equipments, 1800–1941* Osprey, 1983
Chappell, Mike *British infantry equipments, 1808–1908* Osprey, 1980
Davis, Brian L. *British army uniforms and insignia of World War Two* Arms & Armour Press, 1983
Fosten, D.S.V. and Marrion, R.J. *The British Army, 1914–1918* Osprey, 1978
Jewell, Brian *British battledress, 1937–1961* Osprey, 1981
Lawson, Cecil C.P. *A history of the uniforms of the British Army, Volumes I – V* P. Davies, 1940–1967
Smith, D.G. *The British Army, 1965–80* Osprey, 1977
Wise, Terence *Artillery equipments of the Napoleonic Wars* Osprey, 1979

WEAPONS

Bailey, De Witt *British military longarms 1715–1865* Arms & Armour Press, 1986
Bidwell, Shelford and Graham, Dominick *Firepower: British Army weapons and theories of war 1904–1945* Allen & Unwin, 1982
Blackmore, Howard L. *British military firearms, 1650–1850* Herbert Jenkins, 1961
Caldwell, D. (Ed.) *Scottish weapons and fortifications, 1100–1800* John Donald, 1981
Ellis, John *The social history of the machine gun* Croom Helm, 1975
Hobart, F.W.A. *Pictorial history of the machine gun* Ian Allan, 1971
Roads, C.H. *The British soldier's firearm, 1850–1864* Herbert Jenkins, 1964
Robson, Brian *Swords of the British Army: the regulation patterns, 1788–1914* Arms & Armour Press, 1975
Wallace, John *Scottish swords and dirks: an illustrated reference guide to Scottish edged weapons* Arms & Armour Press, 1970

BIBLIOGRAPHIES

Bruce, A.P.C. *An annotated bibliography of the British Army, 1660–1914* Garland, 1975
Higham, Robin (Ed.) *A guide to the sources of British military history*, Routledge & Kegan Paul, 1972
White, Arthur S. *A bibliography of regimental histories of the British Army* Society for Army Historical Research, 1965

ACKNOWLEDGEMENTS FOR PHOTOGRAPHS

Her Majesty The Queen 49, Colour picture 7.

National Museums of Scotland 1–3, 6–9, 11–15, 18, 20, 27–29B, 31–36, 43–45, 50–56, 58–63, 65–67, 69–71, 73–121, 125–127, 131–132, 137–163, 170–175, 181, 186, 190, 202–205, 210, 212–220, 224–240, 257, colour pictures 4, 5, 11–29, 31.

National Army Museum, London 16, 17, 47, 48.

The Livrustkammaren, Stockholm Colour pictures 2, 3.

4th Royal Tank Regiment Colour Picture 30.

Scottish National Portrait Gallery 24–26, 40, 41, Colour Picture 9.

National Portrait Gallery, London 21, 22, 38, 39, Colour Pictures 5, 6.

The National Galleries of Scotland Colour Picture 10.

The Scottish Development Department 5, 46, Colour Pictures 1, 8.

The Master and Fellows of Corpus Christi College, Cambridge 10

The British Library 19

Perth Museum and Art Gallery 30

His Grace the Duke of Atholl 42

Smithsonian Institution Washington D.C. 64.

Tom Scott, Edinburgh 68

Imperial War Museum 122, 123, 128, 133–135, 143B, 143C, 164–168, 176–180, 182–185B, 187–189B, 191–201, 206–209B, 211, 221–223B, 241, 250–256.

Derby Evening Telegraph 242–244.

Ministry of Defence (Army) 245–249.

EDINBURG